Making the most of
KITCHENS & DINING ROOMS

Making the most of

KITCHENS & DINING ROOMS

MARY GILLIATT

A creative guide to home design

Orbis Publishing, London

Original room designs created by Mary Gilliatt
and illustrated by Ross Wardle/Tudor Art Studios

Special photography by Jon Bouchier and Jessica Strang

Copyright © 1983 Orbis Publishing Limited
Text copyright © 1983 by Mary Gilliatt
Second impression 1983

First published in Great Britain
by Orbis Publishing Limited, London 1983

Printed in Italy

ISBN 0 85613 556 9

CONTENTS

If kitchens are the most complicated rooms to plan they are also the most rewarding to get right, for we spend a large part of our lives by the stove and sink. The kitchen is above all a working room and although good looks are an integral part of its design, easy function should be the prime consideration. If it is a machine for cooking, as design writers are fond of saying, it must be a well oiled one.

A kitchen tends to fall into one of three categories depending on its physical limitations and your life pattern: it may be designed purely as a work room when all the other family activities go on in other rooms; or it may be a room where the work is done and some or all family meals are taken; or finally it may be the real centre of the house, where work is done, meals are taken and where the family congregates.

Over the decades since the First World War, with the introduction of new forms of energy, the development of labour saving devices and changes in food and menus, there have been radical changes in kitchen design. By the 1950s, designers had turned kitchens into streamlined boxes with aseptic, clinical, easily wipeable finishes. It looked as if all traces of the cluttered, lived-in, homey kitchen, the heart and hearth of the home, had gone for ever. The appliance manufacturers, the frozen food kings, the canners and food merchants exploited to the hilt the female desire to get out of the kitchen just as quickly as possible.

But that was before the great cooking revolution which has restored the kitchen as a family room, if not *the* family room: warm, friendly, relaxed and comfortable. Nevertheless, if it's going to work at all, a well planned kitchen has, first and foremost, to suit the cook.

Given all this, a book about kitchens and kitchen decoration would be illogical to say the least, if it failed to take into account the room or area where food is served, which should be as pleasant a place as possible. Not only is the one space the inevitable extension of the other, but as often as not these days, the kitchen and dining areas are in the same room anyway. Today's dining rooms are defined by *where* you eat, not by the furniture. How you arrange these cooking/eating functions in your home depends on your life style as well as the space and money available.

Unless you have ample funds to hand, it is of the utmost importance to think ahead when you are planning a kitchen. You might not be able to afford all the appliances you would like from the start, but if you think you will need them and will be able to afford them later you must leave the space and supply utilities for them. That is to say, if you want a dishwasher but know you won't be able to afford one for, say, three years, then make sure the plumbing is available and that there is a niche for a new fixture before you install your worktops and units.

If you are planning on a family and intending to stay in your present home, then allow for much more storage space than you need now. And whatever your current needs, try to get as much worktop or counter space as you possibly can. You always need far more dumping/preparation areas than you could ever imagine.

Finally, make sure that you have ample power points or outlets. They are much easier to fit earlier than later; wires can be more easily concealed and circuits worked out at the start of kitchen planning. Again, you will probably need more than you think at first reckoning. Start thinking along the right lines from the very beginning.

The main point of this book is to give ideas allied to practical information. But to get the most from ideas or information you will have to know how they can best be applied to your own particular situation and circumstances.

Compact, practical and stylish – this kitchen with dining area has all the ingredients which make it as attractive a place in which to eat as it is to prepare food.

If you are in the happy position of being able to plan your kitchen from scratch, rather than attempting to re-vamp existing layouts and equip-ment, it is worth giving the matter considerable thought.

It may even happen that you are able to choose *where* your kitchen will be, in which case bear in mind the following criteria. If your dining room is to be separate from your kitchen there should ideally be easy access from one room to the other. Long passages or stairs between the two make for difficulties in keeping food hot and clearing tables. Ease of access to the garden, especial-ly if you grow your own herbs, vegetables and fruit, is also important, as is min-imising the time you spend answering the front and back doors. Good natural daylight and attractive views are less im-portant but should certainly be taken into consideration.

Once you have decided where you want your kitchen the next decision to make is what sort of kitchen you want. This will depend very much on what sort of cook you are. If you entertain a lot you may well prefer to have your kitchen separate from the dining area, unless you opt for a large and deliberately-for-dining kitchen. A dedicated cook with a demanding job outside the home will probably need their kitchen to be that much more func-tional than someone with more leisure to shop – at least in the sense of providing good storage and extra-quick cooking facilities, such as a microwave oven and a freezer.

A single person, or a couple without children, extremely busy and not overly fond of cooking will almost certainly prefer a functional, working room that looks and is efficient.

If you really enjoy cooking you will pro-bably want to be able to take at least some meals in the kitchen and to have as much space as possible for herbs, spices, pots and pans, cook books and all the other impedimenta collected by the keen cook, quite apart from generous food storage and good kitchen aids.

If you cook constantly, have a

The sort of kitchen on the left would be ideal for some people with its generous work surfaces, storage and uncluttered feel. Others, especially dedicated cooks, might prefer the wood finishes and general organized chaos (right) of a room that is basically the same shape but arranged differently.

family and are forced to spend a lot of time in the kitchen, you will probably want to make it much more of a family room where people can sit around and talk, have a drink, do their homework, write notes, lists, letters, pay bills, and do a lot of eating.

Fit your space to your life style
If you are not quite sure of the sort of kitchen that will best suit you, ask yourself the following questions:

⬤ Do you think your present situation will remain static or are you likely to have children and more children (their friends), guests and more guests to feed in the ensuing years?

⬤ Do you know what kind of meals you are most likely to cook, for how many, and how often? (Remember that the *kind* of cooking you do is very much to the point, for if you only cook simple meals you will need far less preparation area than a more ambitious cook – though here again your aspirations may change with experience.)

⬤ Do you work all day, and are you likely to go on doing so?

⬤ Do you live far from a good shopping area so that you will need more than the average amount of food storage space and a large deep freeze?

⬤ Even if you cannot afford them now, are you likely to acquire extra equipment in the future like a dishwasher, microwave oven, washing machine or freezer?

⬤ Will there be more than one of you cooking or working in the kitchen at any one time? Kitchens that work really well for one, very seldom do for two (or more).

⬤ Are you lucky enough to possess space for a utility or washing room? If so, you can hive off washing machine, dryers, ironing equipment and probably cleaning appliances and accessories, which is a great help when you are short of space.

⬤ All these points should be thought about and considered in relation to the space you have to play with (a square room, rectangular room, cramped galley, and so on) as well as any existing appliances, and should certainly give you a clearer idea of the sort of room that will answer your needs.

What do you need? What can you afford?
Having decided that point, you should next make a list of the kitchen furniture and utensils that you would like, if not now, then later when you can better afford them so that you can plan your kitchen around specific objects.

The suggested *batterie de cuisine* should act as a point of reference. Write down the items you need: for the major items, make a note of the makes you would like, the price, and the dimensions, if relevant. Work out how much storage you will need for smaller pieces of equipment, serving equipment and foodstuffs: will one shelf in a cupboard be enough for tins, or do you need several? Can you hang saucepans on the wall near the cooker, or do you need cupboards or drawers for them? Will serving dishes, cutlery, table linen be kept in the kitchen or is there space for them near the dining table? Does cleaning and washing equipment have to live in the kitchen, or is there a utility room/cupboard under the stairs, or even a large bathroom where they can be stored?

Left: This purpose-built kitchen/dining/living room is unashamedly utilitarian, clean-cut and neat. It is also quite luxurious with its built-in tv and stereo units vying for place with rather more normal kitchen equipment.

Right: There is a totally different feel to this multi-purpose space viewed from the kitchen area. The kitchen equipment and utensils are used as homely decoration while a sofa and chairs provide comfortable seating in the living/dining area.

FIRST MAKE YOUR PLANS

Batterie de cuisine

When it comes to cooking and serving a meal, everyone has slightly different techniques and habits. There can be no hard and fast rules as to what is essential, and what is a real luxury: some people are happy to make do with microwave ovens and electric frying pans, and not to use conventional cookers, while others will have no more than a cooker and fridge in the way of electrical/gas appliances.

The following batterie de cuisine (list of kitchen equipment) is divided into basics, optionals and luxuries. The basics are the absolute minimum, to give you a guide as to what will be needed if you are starting from scratch. You will probably need to allow room for the items on the optional lists, and certainly you should consider the luxuries – which you may or may not need, according to space, life style and cooking and eating habits.

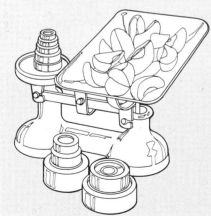

	Essential basics	Optional extras	Specialised luxuries
Appliances	Cooker: free-standing, built-under worktop or separate built-in oven(s) and hob Refrigerator	Freezer Washing machine Cooker hood/extractor fan	Microwave Dishwasher Dryer (tumble or spin)
	Kettle	Toaster Beater/mixer/blender/ grinder/food processor Slow cooker Coffee maker	Sandwich maker Infra-red/contact grill Electric frying pan Chip fryer Electric carving knife Ice cream maker Soft drink maker
Preparation and cooking	Set of saucepans Frying pan Casserole Baking tray Cake tins Roasting tin Mixing bowls Sieve Colander Set of knives: vegetable, cook's knife, carving knife, bread knife Wooden spoons Slotted spoon Fish slice Grater Knife sharpener Egg whisk (rotary or wire) Scissors Corkscrew Can opener Chopping board Oven gloves Apron Rolling pin Scales/weighing machine	Extra casserole and pans Chip pan Pressure cooker Steamer Omelette pan Extra cake tins and patty pans Roasting rack Cake rack Range of sieves and strainers Freezer knife, boning knife, meat cleaver, extra vegetable and cook's knives Potato peeler Wooden spatula Potato masher Ladles Large spoons Jelly moulds Skewers, kebab sticks Pastry board Funnel Meat tenderiser Measuring jug Potato baking spike Flan dishes	Preserving pan Jelly bag Crêpe pan Cast iron grill Bread tins Meat and jam thermometers Grapefruit knife Copper bowl Twig whisk Larding needle Trussing needles Bulb baster Set of measuring spoons Ice cream scoop Pasta making equipment Beer and wine making equipment

Essential basics	Optional extras	Specialised luxuries
	Pie dishes	
	Soufflé dishes	
	Garlic press (with olive/cherry stoner)	
	Icing equipment	
	Piping bag and nozzles	

Serving

Essential basics	Optional extras	Specialised luxuries
Plates: dinner and side	Breakfast plates	Fish knives and forks
Bowls for soup, dessert or cereals	Extra bowls for soup, dessert etc.	Steak knives
Cups and saucers	Soup spoons	Cocktail, liqueur, port and brandy glasses
Egg cups	Sherry, red/white wine glasses	Special individual dishes for avocado, corn on the cob, scallops, snails, asparagus, artichoke, small ramekins, etc.
Mugs	Extra serving dishes and platters	
Teapot	Coffee cups	
Jug	Coffee pot	
Cruets (preferably mills)	Large and small jugs	Fondue set
Knives, forks, dessert spoons, teaspoons	Glass jug	
	Carafe	
Serving spoons	Gravy boat	
Wine glasses	Cheese board	
Tumblers	Butter dish	
Serving bowls	Toast rack	
Salad bowls and servers	Table linen	
Meat dish	Trays	
Bread board		
Table mats		

Cleaning

Essential basics	Optional extras	Specialised luxuries
Sink with draining board	Second sink	Waste disposal unit
Broom	Draining rack	Water softener
Dustpan and brush	Vacuum cleaner	Electric polisher
Waste bin	Carpet sweeper (manual)	Carpet shampooer
Bucket	Ironing board	Rotary iron
Floor cloth	Scrubbing brush	
Washing up mop/sponge	Clothes airer	
Tea towels		
Duster/polishing cloths		
Iron		

Once you have worked out what items you will eventually need, consider how and where to store them. In addition to this equipment, you will need to find storage space for the following: Bread; cakes and biscuits; dry goods—pasta, rice, flour, fruit, pulses, sugar, tea, coffee; condiments—sauces, relishes, jams etc; vegetables; tinned goods; home-made preserves; cookery books; empty freezer/fridge storage containers and cleaning materials

Left: A satisfactory 'work-triangle' is formed by refrigerator, sink and stove in this awkwardly-shaped kitchen. Forethought and good planning has produced a room which is attractive to work in, well equipped, labour-saving and ergonomically sound.

Above: Neat and perfectly adequate cooking space for a couple has been squeezed into this compact and corridor-like area.

When you have completed your list, think about the basic services you will need: how many electrical appliances are on the list? Where will each one be plugged in? New tracking devices are coming on to the market to make this stage of planning easier, but most of us still have to plan where we want our socket outlets and lighting long before any kitchen equipment can be installed.

It might sound elementary, but it is only too easy to leave out quite obvious necessities in the trauma of getting everything done and easier still to discount the quite alarming final costs. This way, you can at least work out the essentials and plan from there.

How to plan your space
The chief rule for any successful kitchen plan is that it should always follow a work diagram based on the sequence of operations. Because food preparation generally involves a good deal of doubling back to and from the refrigerator, sink, stove and different work surfaces, the walking distance between all the main work areas should not be excessive. And each work area needs careful thought to ensure that all necessary equipment and ingredients are conveniently to hand.

The three principal work areas—preparation, cooking and washing-up—are centred on the fridge, the cooker and the sink. Professional kitchen planners use the term 'work triangle' to describe the imaginary lines linking the three areas. While you must allow enough space in each area to work efficiently, they must not be spaced too far apart, or you will be walking backwards and forwards much more than is necessary.

Consider the operation involved in cooking something as simple as frozen peas:

1 Take pan to sink and fill.
2 Take pan to cooker. Add salt. Bring to boil.
3 Remove peas from refrigerator. Open bag with scissors. Add to pan. Discard bag.
4 When cooked, take pan to sink. Use colander to strain.
5 Tip peas into serving dish.
6 Get butter from refrigerator. Use knife to add a knob of butter.
7 Return butter to fridge. Put dirty utensils in sink or dishwasher.
8 Take peas to table.

Even a task as simple as this involves two trips to the sink, three trips to the refrigerator, and two trips to the cooker (more if you warmed the serving dish first). You also need to visit the cupboards and drawers where the pan, salt, scissors, knife and colander are kept, and dispose of the bag in the rubbish bin.

So the distances between the work areas are crucial: each side of the work triangle should be between 1250 and 2150 mm (4–7 ft). If its perimeter is more than 6.6 m (22 ft) you will be walking around more than necessary. If it is less than 4 m (13 ft) you won't have enough room to be able to manoeuvre yourself comfortably.

You must organize your storage around the work areas according to what is needed: knives near the preparation area; spices between the preparation and cooking areas; wooden spoons near the cooker; coffee, tea and mugs near the kettle and so on. It may not be possible to get everything precisely where you want it, so think about the things you do most often (such as making a cup of tea, cooking a casserole) or in most of a hurry (preparing breakfast) and try to make the work flow for these tasks as simple and streamlined as possible.

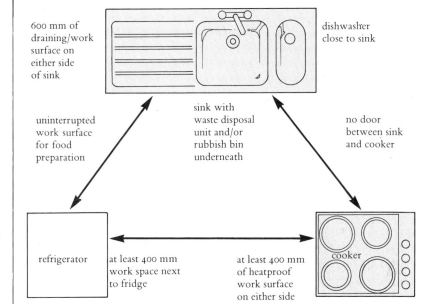

600 mm of draining/work surface on either side of sink

dishwasher close to sink

uninterrupted work surface for food preparation

sink with waste disposal unit and/or rubbish bin underneath

no door between sink and cooker

refrigerator

at least 400 mm work space next to fridge

at least 400 mm of heatproof work surface on either side

cooker

The 'work-triangle'
In the ideal kitchen, sink, cooker and refrigerator are spaced evenly apart from one another to form a compact work triangle. Unfortunately this is not always easy to achieve as windows, irregular walls and limited space need to be taken into account. You will find some examples of typical solutions in Chapter 3.

wooden slats proud of wall used to store decorative equipment

adjustable clip-on spot over work area

attractive red mixer tap

flue painted red to make a feature

fluorescent strip behind fascia board

butcher-block work surface

rubbish bin on back of unit door

extractor fan over hob

non-slip Pirelli flooring

Slatted wooden walls take care of a massed batterie de cuisine in this all-wood kitchen. Hooks can simply be fed through the gaps. Less attractive pieces of kitchen equipment are cleverly concealed behind matching fascia panels.

central heating boiler concealed by matching fascia panel

Put it on paper

Obviously, the actual dimensions of your particular work triangle are going to be determined by the basic floor plan of your kitchen. So you need to draw up a plan of what you've got already, then you can work out how best to improve it. This is the procedure to follow, whether you're planning a new kitchen entirely from scratch, or re-organizing an existing one.

You will need some graph paper, a tape measure, a sharp pencil, ruler and eraser. Measure the room's dimensions (length and width, allowing exactly the right space for doors, windows, breaks in walls, structural columns, radiators, fixtures and so on) and draw them out to scale making sure that they are absolutely exact. The slightest error can be disastrous when you have to fit in appliances and units. If you have awkward pipes, low windows, a hatch or power points already in position, mark them on the plan, and measure up and draw elevations of the walls as well.

Measure up any items which have to stay in the kitchen, and cut out shapes from graph paper to represent them. If they can't be moved (for example you may prefer not to call in a plumber to move the sink), stick them down. Try to be as flexible as possible: it may be well worth moving, say, the cooker as little as 1 metre (3 ft) from its existing position

in order to create a better work flow. Play around with the shapes and don't stick things down on your plan unless you are sure they can't be moved.

Work out the best way to organize your work triangle, then connect the points of the triangle. If the triangle does not seem as efficient as professional planners would like, see if you can move the appliances or work surfaces to give a better arrangement. For example, to increase working and manoeuvring space in an existing work triangle you could set up a second food preparation or cooking area with perhaps a microwave oven outside your main work area. To lessen the distance between, say, the refrigerator and the sink, you could add an island unit to the centre of the room, or a free-standing butcher-block work surface, or even a mobile work trolley.

Your particular triangle may well be unique, as it results from a combination of your particular space, and your particular needs. But there are some standard arrangements which may give you some helpful ideas. You can look at these in more detail in Chapter 3.

Once you have traced out your basic floor plan and work triangle you can develop the rest of the kitchen to include more work space (like a pastry or baking preparation area), more storage, other appliances, an eating area (if there's

room), perhaps a desk area, and look into more technical details like electric outlets, and lighting. Finally, you will be able to add the finishing touches with decoration. If you cannot do everything at once, or want to start making staged improvements, either concentrate on your first priorities (leaving space for the next stages) or your worst problems – depending on whether you are planning a first-time kitchen or updating an existing one.

Corridor or galley kitchens are often particularly easy to work in – as long as there are not more than two people. This one is a model of its kind with clean lines, red and white scheme, wire grid hanging areas and careful use of every bit of space. Note the shelves across the window and over the door. Vivid red sinks, red and white checked vinyl flooring, red-topped stools, and fine red edging to the door frame to match the accessories, all contribute to the scheme.

Basic kitchen with big ideas

With a little ingenuity you can make a perfectly adequate and cheerful kitchen on the smallest of budgets in the most awkward of spaces. This room has a low and sloping ceiling and very little natural light yet manages to look airy, bright and well-equipped even though the only appliances are the most basic models of sink, stove and fridge. There are no units and very little equipment apart from the versatile wok. With such a low ceiling and lack of light the first priority was lighting—achieved with inset eyeball spots. There was no money for tiles but walls and ceiling were covered in a red and white check paper given a toughening coat of clear eggshell polyurethane. Appliances were linked by a run of white laminate work top which formed a counter at one end. This serves as an eating bar now but later can accommodate a dishwasher. In the absence of wall units storage is taken care of by red plastic coated open shelving, open shelving built into the recess and cupboard with home-hung louvre doors. The floor is covered with red and white sheet vinyl in a smaller square design. The detailing is completed by the red taps, red handles on the cupboard under the sink and the pullout red vegetable baskets on wheels.

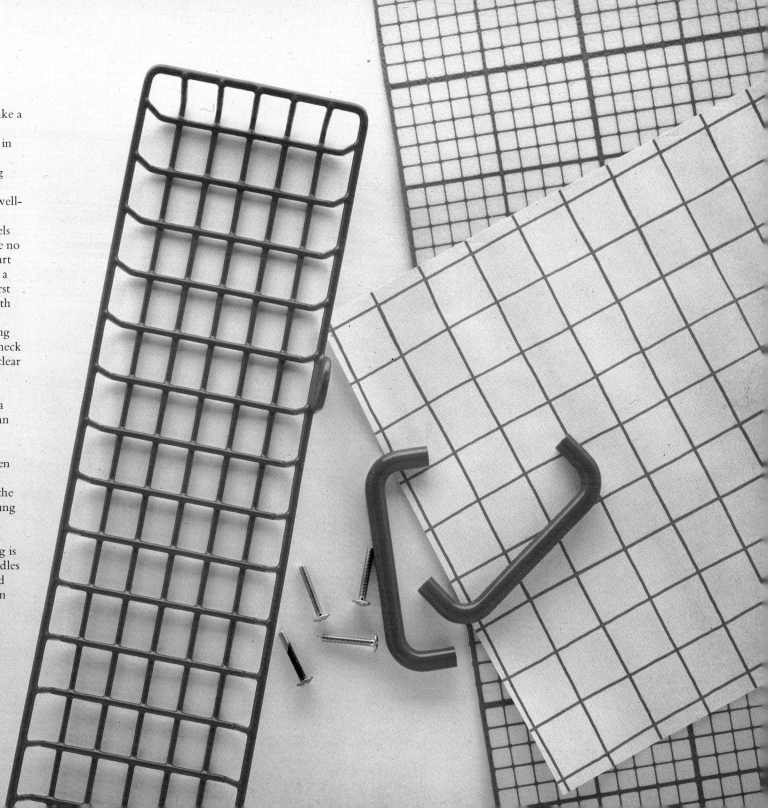

FIRST MAKE YOUR PLANS

The importance of lighting

The same rules for planning light fittings apply in the kitchen as everywhere else in the home: general light to see by; work light to work by; an accent light to show off anything particularly worth looking at. The special rule of the kitchen is to make sure that there is light over every work surface so that you never work in your own shadow.

Insert general pendant lighting or inset downlights or wallwashers for the overall light; fix baffled light below cabinets to shine directly onto the worktop, and try to install special lights over stove and sink. If you are going to eat in the kitchen make sure overall lights are on a dimmer switch and that there is enough light over the table—use a rise-and-fall light fixture for example—which can, of course, be substituted for or combined with candlelight at night. Independent switches for each light will make it easier to create the appropriate atmosphere.

Fluorescent tubes are best for under cabinet/worktop lighting. They last much longer than incandescent tubes, offer more light per watt but need to be carefully chosen in the right colours for the most accurate presentation of food. That is to say, choose warm white de luxe (not just warm white) or cool white de luxe (not just cool white). There is no point in dimming fluorescent

Top left: Lighting, albeit slightly unconventional, is placed exactly where it matters in this kitchen; that is over the cook top and over the work surface, where spotlights are intertwined through a suspended wire grid.

Left: A square of centrally-placed tubular track has mobile spotlights trained on all the relevant parts of the kitchen as well as on the sink and grill area immediately underneath.

Above: In this deliberately old-fashioned and eclectic-style room with its prettily stencilled walls, a series of pendant lights is hung above the butcher block and dining table.

light; although it is possible, it is extremely costly and unnecessary. Mount tubes as close to the front of cabinets as possible and shield them with a baffle or small valance or cornice attached to the bottom of units. This will subdue any glare.

Sinks will need a minimum of two 100 watt incandescent bulbs or two 75 watt reflector floodlights which will focus light directly onto the bowls and draining boards.

If you have a hood over your hob or stove you should see that bulbs are enclosed to protect them from spattered grease and heat. Most manufacturers recommend a 60 watt maximum; or use fluorescent tubes.

Island work areas can be lit by general light, a rise-and-fall fixture or a fluorescent fixture containing at least two 30 or 40 watt tubes. Alternatively, try recessed or surface-mounted downlights using, say, 75 watt reflector floods. Good results for considerably less money can be achieved with clamp-on work lights.

Almost all light sources are concealed in the working area of this good-looking Hi-Tech kitchen. The exception – the long tubular green-cased fluorescent suspended from the ceiling – is as much sculptural decoration as lighting fixture. Note the large green-painted galvanized steel extractor fan over the cook top and supporting green columns.

If you find your kitchen hard to work in, tiring, cramped for space, uninspiring, or shabby, you can at least take comfort in the fact that you are not alone. The trouble is that the majority of kitchens in the majority of homes were designed years ago with appliances, storage cabinets, work surfaces and lighting that is now either inadequate or unsuitable. Alternatively it may be that your kitchen actually functions with great efficiency and is relatively modern but simply lacks character. Whatever the problem, there is always a solution, so long as you are prepared to use your ingenuity, be flexible and remember that rules were made to be broken—or at least bent a little.

Unfortunately some solutions rely on structural changes for effect, but these don't always have to involve vast expense. For example, if you are short of wall space and have a door off the kitchen leading to a room which can also be approached from another door, block off the kitchen door. This could either involve removing it altogether and blocking up the space with bricks and mortar, or simply locking it and putting furniture against it on both sides.

Similarly, if your problem is one of poor ventilation leading to a steamy or smoke-filled room in which it is difficult to see anything, the solution is obviously an air extractor. This could be let into the wall, which would mean taking up valuable wall space and also involving duct work. You could, however, if there is a window in the room, replace a pane of glass with one heavy enough to resist the weight and pressure of an air extractor. This will save on time, convenience and expense. If more drastic action is called for, some alternatives are outlined in Chapter 3.

It may be that all that is required is a little lateral thinking. For example, if you are short of storage space, a perennial complaint, perhaps you should consider the ceiling. You would be amazed at what can be stored at this level. A high ceiling is, of course, a prerequisite if you wish to avoid constantly banging your head.

The charmingly rustic kitchen on the left could scarcely be called custom-built; but it does have good storage facilities and refreshing touches like the window frames. Even more decorative treatment has been given to the all-wood kitchen on the right.

ROOM FOR IMPROVEMENT

Luckily, as most of us have neither the money nor the time to undertake major remodelling, it is quite possible to make significant changes without going to the bank for a loan or calling in a builder.

If you have not really thought how you could improve your space, or can't quite place what is wrong, ask yourself the following questions:

● Do you find you are walking around a lot, even to prepare the simplest of meals?

● Do you always seem to be shifting things along on your worktops in order to make room to prepare something?

● Do you have to keep looking for things? A particular knife perhaps, or some other essential-at-the-time utensil?

● Are you constantly having to move things around in your cabinet in order to find what you need?

● Are all your cupboards or closets crammed full?

● Can you see items on your shelves or in your cabinets which you have not used for at least a year?

● Has the size of your household changed since the last time you bought a kitchen appliance?

● Do people tend to stand around in your kitchen when they are eating a snack or drinking the odd cup of coffee because there is no place to sit?

● Is your kitchen the sort of place where family and friends congregate for chats as a matter of course. If not, would you like it to be?

● Would you like to change the whole look but don't think you have the money?

● Are you in rented property so feel you just have to put up with what you have?

If you have answered yes to at least three of these questions, some sort of change is certainly due, if not overdue. Here's how to achieve it.

The answer to the first problem is obviously to try to do something about your domestic traffic problems. If you do seem to be walking around a lot during meal preparations try to count the number of times you walk to various work areas and even the number of steps you take. You might well find that another work counter will help a good deal. If there is no room to add any extra counter space try importing a free-standing butcher-block worktop or a trolley or cart. Again, if you find you are always walking back and forth to a larder or pantry, or to shelves at the other end of the kitchen, a storage trolley or cart which you could wheel up when necessary should help.

Far left: A free-standing butcher-block worktop adds useful extra working space in just the right area. The walls, stripped down to the bare brick, could accept more shelves in the future. The use of light wood on all surfaces unifies the eclectic mixture.

Left: Extra pull-out worktops have been built in to this run of units. The deep pelmet adds interest.

Above: More storage and workspace, complete with integral steps, have been provided here by a kind of kitchen 'tower'. A further space-saving idea is the white-painted sliding door with its sculptural hanging chair.

Ringing the changes

However good-looking a room might seem there is nothing like day-to-day use to point up its shortcomings. The drawbacks of this dining-kitchen were soon realised to be lack of storage and worktop space and the hardness and noisiness of the otherwise splendid brick floor. The easiest solutions were to build storage around the large window and to cover the floor with coir matting—softer underfoot than bare brick but tough and hard-wearing. To keep the general character of the room a pine unit was built to the same size and style of the old dresser base which formed the original worktop and storage units. Its tiled top was replaced with solid butcher block and this was continued onto the new unit. A butcher-block trolley/cart added extra work space. The window shutters were removed and glass shelves and a rod were hung right across the panes to hold herbs, plants and pots, pans and implements. On one side of the window there was room for a capacious wooden cabinet, matched on the other side by a pine bookshelf unit about the same size. This takes all the cook books. The old beige cotton chair cushions were re-covered in a green Provençal print and teamed with a flower bordered tablecloth in another print. The result is a very pleasing kitchen which also works well.

ROOM FOR IMPROVEMENT

Make good use of storage space. Top left: Industrial shelving and wire grid have been used to excellent effect in this Hi-Tech kitchen. Above: Almost every surface except the window has been utilised here for storage. Far left: This storage unit pulls out on wheels to reveal pots and pans. The painted outlines make quick replacement easy. Left: A plate drying rack and storage shelves suspended over the sink.

Sensible storage

Several more of the problems are clearly to do with your current storage or methods of storage. People are always complaining that they do not have enough work space/dumping space, but it may well be what they really need is better organized storage. Look at the work spaces at your disposal. Are you using them to their best advantage? Or are they so cluttered up that there isn't any real space to work on? If clutter is your only problem, be ruthless and get rid of anything hanging around that you have not used for the last six months, and put anything else away in a cupboard, cabinet or closet somewhere.

If there does not seem any room to get rid of storage jars, canisters, cook tools and so on, you might need to add more shelves and hooks. You can often use the space between the bottom of wall-hung cabinets and the counter top to put up small shelves which will take a variety of objects; this is often a good place to stand your collection of dried herbs in small pots or jars—it keeps them together, clearly visible and to hand. And if you add cup hooks to the edges you can hang things from them as well. Another useful extra storage space is behind cabinet doors where again you might fix narrow shelves or hooks. And don't overlook the exposed sides of end base or wall-hung cabinets.

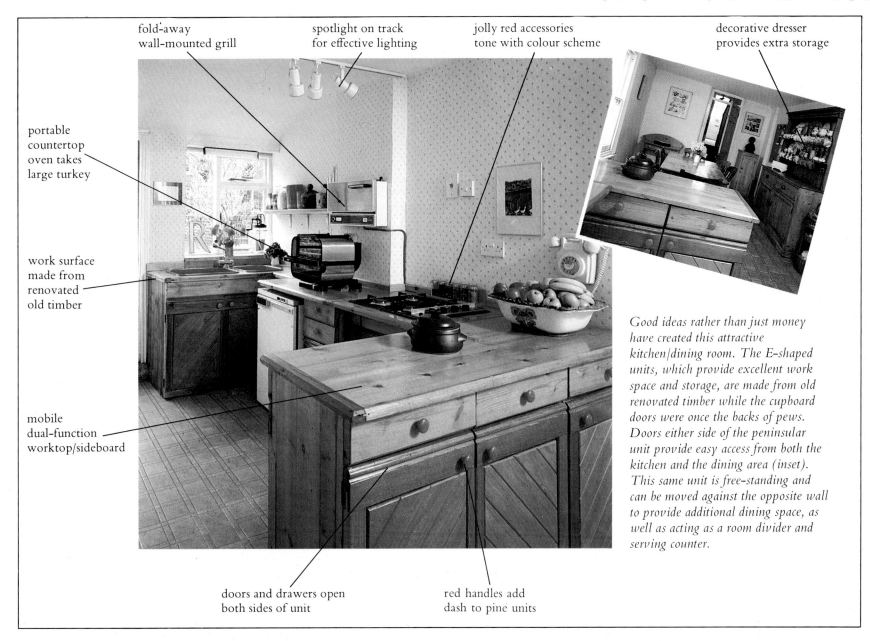

fold-away
wall-mounted grill

spotlight on track
for effective lighting

jolly red accessories
tone with colour scheme

decorative dresser
provides extra storage

portable
countertop
oven takes
large turkey

work surface
made from
renovated
old timber

mobile
dual-function
worktop/sideboard

doors and drawers open
both sides of unit

red handles add
dash to pine units

Good ideas rather than just money have created this attractive kitchen/dining room. The E-shaped units, which provide excellent work space and storage, are made from old renovated timber while the cupboard doors were once the backs of pews. Doors either side of the peninsular unit provide easy access from both the kitchen and the dining area (inset). This same unit is free-standing and can be moved against the opposite wall to provide additional dining space, as well as acting as a room divider and serving counter.

Streamlined surfaces

A quick way to re-vamp a tired looking kitchen is to re-cover or replace the work surface.

Butcher-block, though expensive, will turn your food preparation area into one long chopping board. Oil it frequently, sand it occasionally and it will last for years. But avoid using it near the sink (where it might warp or the surface might rise) or close to the cooker (unless you have tiles and trivets for hot pans).

Tiles are a popular choice in country-style kitchens, but not to be recommended if you are heavy-handed with pots and pans. You can lay them on chipboard or plywood, or use them to cover your existing work surface. Rub down the surface with glasspaper, stick the tiles down with a suitable adhesive and grout in between them with a synthetic plastic bathroom or kitchen sealant (which won't pick up stains). Or use special coloured pigment (food colouring works too) to darken it. Edge the new surface with wooden beading, painted or varnished to suit the style of the kitchen.

If you have access to woodworking equipment or are employing a handyman, you can use planks of beech or hardwood, butted together and edged with rounded beading. Give the surface at least three coats of yacht varnish, rubbing down lightly with wire wool between coats.

Plastic laminate surfaces can be renewed: round-edged surfaces will have to be taken out and replaced. Square-edged surfaces can be re-covered with laminate, using edging strips of the same material, or lipping the edge with wooden beading.

If your kitchen is made up of separate units, each with its own worktop, you may be able to get a more streamlined look by installing a long run of worktop joining the separate units. If the units don't match the length of the wall, you can create a tray or vegetable storage area by leaving a space between units or continuing the worktop beyond the end of the unit, butting it up to the wall.

A cheerful but cheap way to renovate a worktop is to cover it with self-adhesive plastic, like Fablon. Smooth it tightly over the work surface, then give it a couple of coats of polyurethane for protection. It won't be as tough as plastic laminate, but it will be fairly hardwearing.

Many professional kitchens have stainless steel work surfaces, with wooden chopping blocks and marble sections (for pastry making) let into them. But stainless steel is expensive, and unless it is properly cushioned underneath it can be very noisy.

A complete work surface in marble would be impractical: cold, hard and expensive. But it might be worth topping one part of your work area (a single unit or a free-standing refrigerator) with marble for pastry making. But remember that it is easily stained by wine, acids and lemon juice.

Synthetic marble is an alternative: Corian is a new material for work surfaces which is proof against most stains, reasonably heat resistant, non-porous, and cuts like wood.

Sealed cork flooring tiles may also be used to re-cover a surface, but like butcher-block, they are not suitable for areas exposed to great heat or water.

Slate is useful for pastry-making and also provides a decorative top.

Pale butcher-block makes a most elegant counter in this handsome room.

This Corian worktop comes complete with good-looking recessed sinks.

Extra work space

If you are satisfied that you have spirited away all possible clutter and still do not have adequate preparation space you could cover a sink with a portable chopping board, or turn a drawer into an extra work surface by fitting runners to a block of wood the same width as the drawer, so that it will glide in and out of the unit, resting on the top of the drawer when it is pulled out.

Cleaned up cupboards

If your cabinets seem to be constantly overcrowded, open up all the doors and look at the contents with a critical eye. If there are items around that you hardly ever use, remove them to more remote storage areas away from your work areas. Seldom used or once-a-year items like ham boiling pans, turkey roasting pans, fish kettles, picnic baskets etc, might well be parted from the day-to-day items. Or you can hang pot racks from the ceiling; and put up areas of peg boards to hang colanders, sieves, whisks, graters and so on.

If you have not bought any new appliances since you first moved into your home, or if your family has changed in numbers, you might well be due for some updated versions. The sort of choice available is explained fully in Chapter 4, but a new refrigerator or fridge-freezer, the addition of a microwave oven, or the purchase of a portable dishwasher if

there is no room for a plumbed-in version, might make all the difference to your own work load.

Another salient question to ask yourself is: are you really using your space to its best advantage. I am not talking here about your work surfaces, or work triangles or the general space/work efficiency of your kitchen, but rather if you could use your kitchen as more of a family room—the sort of room which friends as well as family tend to migrate to at the first available opportunity. Obviously this is not relevant if you have a tiny galley kitchen, or a slit of corridor space, but if you can add a chair or two, or at least a couple of stools where there were none before; and some sort of bar, or at least an enlarged counter top if you can't fit in a decent table, then you are well on the way to making your kitchen a more welcoming place.

Another kitchen where every surface is made to work to maximum advantage. The counter top provides space for eating as well as cooking and preparation. Baskets, bowls and a fish kettle are hung on the stone wall. A suspended iron bar just under the ceiling holds a mass of decorative copper pans attached by butcher's hooks. Other walls have hooks for more equipment and still there is room for further expansion, if necessary, along the remaining walls.

You might also think of adding a desk top somewhere: against a small wall; across a corner, as an extension of a worktop. A wooden counter with a couple of filing cabinets underneath, preferably on castors for easy manoeuvrability would be one excellent idea; or just a flip-down panel from a wall would be another. Try and have some shelves above for files and cook books, add a telephone, writing implements and note books, even a typewriter if you can, and you have a mini office to hand whenever you need it.

Finally, you should remember that it really is not necessary to totally re-vamp the kitchen or call in a decorator in order to give it a face lift. There are all sorts of comparatively small changes you can make which will transform your kitchen's looks out of all proportion to the time and expense.

Right: Painted blinds repeat the cherry pattern of the wallpaper and combine with the red accessories to set off the dominant pine.

Left: A compact galley kitchen with many of its original fittings has been given a totally fresh look by painting the units and appliances the background green of the bird-covered wallpaper. Plants enhance the bower image, while pieces of pretty china, paintings, prints and the birdcage inject further charm.

Changes for the better

● Cheer up dull-looking cabinets by painting them in a high gloss or eggshell finish. Or cut a stencil and re-spray the doors adding a simple motif – which can be repeated around the splashback, or around the top of a plain painted room.

● Take off cabinet doors: leave them off altogether for an open shelved look; replace them with new louvred or wooden doors with beading; replace them with glazed doors, or hang curtains in front of shelves instead (PVC fabric curtains won't pick up dirt so easily but cotton is cheaper and easier to wash).

● Re-tile the splashback between counter top and wall-hung cupboards. Plain white tiles are the cheapest: brighten them up with coloured grouting, or mix them with other plain tiles to build up an eye-catching pattern

● Paint everything white: walls, ceiling, units, and add new tiles as well. Even the floor can be painted (see below). The whole place will look amazingly different. Add colour and interest with brightly coloured or prettily patterned kitchen accessories – tea towels, canisters, cook books.

● Cover walls with a vinyl wallpaper (which can be wiped, or even scrubbed), in a pattern to suit your style – an all-over check or floral pattern for a soft, country look; splashy flowers in cheerful colours for a more lively country look; a sharp grid or smart stripe for a more clinical style. If you can't find the pattern you want in a vinyl, you can protect paper wallcoverings with a polyurethane varnish, but it may yellow the pattern slightly.

● Change your window treatment: café curtains instead of a tired roller blind; glass shelves stretched across the window to display bits of china and glass or a collection of old stone and glass bottles; or paint the wooden surround in a pretty colour to frame a crisp new roller blind.

● Either arrange trailing plants such as tradescantia and spider plants in hanging baskets slung from a brass or wooden pole fixed across the window, or intersperse them with herbs and African violets on glass shelves (see above). Some plants like kitchen windows, especially if they are over a steamy sink, but always check first. In a window which does not get much light, a single, showy Boston fern will make a focal point.

● Do the unexpected. 'White goods' (fridge, freezer, washing machine) needn't stay white: re-spray them (in a well-ventilated room) with cans of car paint – by using masking tape you can easily create simple but eye-catching patterns in bold stripes.

ROOM FOR IMPROVEMENT

● Change the walls. Make the room look warm and cheerful by panelling the walls: fix ordinary wooden lathes on the diagonal. Leave them natural or paint them to suit the rest of the decoration. Or cover the walls with tongue-and-groove panelling. Or do away with wallcovering altogether: strip away the plaster to expose the bare brick underneath. (This solution is only suitable for older properties–investigate the structure of the wall in an unobtrusive corner before setting to work.)

● Transform the floor: quarry tile it, or lay new ceramic tiles, Mexican tiles or bricks; put down a well-varnished wood block floor; or lay sheet vinyl, linoleum or vinyl tiles. Sealed cork tiles will create a warm atmosphere. Check the subfloor (is it solid concrete or suspended wood?) before you make your choice, as not all coverings are suitable for all subfloors.

Right: A radical transformation has been achieved in this room by stripping the walls to the brick beneath. The ceiling was tongue-and-grooved, the floor bricked and lights added in the right places.

Top right: Units here were wittily painted to match the upper walls.

Bottom right: Old dresser bases are used instead of modern units.

● For a really economical new floor, add a coat of paint. Liquid Lino is suitable for virtually any surface, and comes in a range of colours. Wood, cork and well-laid vinyl tiles can be painted with gloss paint and given extra protection with a few coats of polyurethane or yacht varnish.

● Add character and charisma: if the room is quite large but lacks personality, simply change some of the existing pieces of furniture: replace the table with an old pine one and add some old pine chairs (available in most junk shops); swap some units for a pine dresser; paint chairs cheerful colours; replace posters with a cork or fabric-covered noticeboard.

● Don't forget details: particularly in rented property, where you can't make substantial alterations, you can still make an enormous difference with carefully chosen accessories: sets of matching storage jars, wooden spice racks, kitchen roll holders, pretty tea towels, bunches of herbs, onions or dried flowers, interesting canisters – old or new; plants; posters; prints; and last, but by no means least, good-looking cookware.

I inherited one kitchen which had lemon yellow units with aluminium knobs, lemon yellow walls, a false flagstone vinyl floor and speckly plastic laminate worktops. I re-moved the units from one short wall, replaced them with a huge old pine dresser and painted all the walls, the ceiling and the rest of the units white. I changed the aluminium knobs for some more cheerful brass handles, covered the wall space between worktops and the bottom of cabinets with some blue and white Mexican tiles (which didn't cost the earth), re-topped the counters with butcher-block and changed the vinyl flagstones for quarry tiles. Result: a total change of character.

For other instant transformations you could jazz up an all-white kitchen say, by adding red and white tiles and red handles, or by just painting a stripe all along between drawers and cupboard doors. Another white kitchen could be given a totally different look by adding green plastic handles and importing masses of plants and some green painted bamboo blinds. Equally you could add wood counter tops to an otherwise all-laminate room, together with wooden slatted blinds, or the plain bamboo or matchstick variety, or some red and white or blue and white check gingham curtains or café curtains.

Once you really start to think of the components that can be changed in a room without too much ado you can come up with any number of ideas for a change of style, or more important, for adding style where none existed before.

When you come to re-vamp your kitchen on a more major scale, your choices are wider. You probably have a good idea of the atmosphere you want to create in your kitchen, and you will find some simplified pointers to style on the following pages. First, however, you have to look at how to make the best use of existing space.

Making sense of your space

The great advantage of starting from scratch in a kitchen is that you can, for very little extra cost, make major improvements by re-positioning services (gas, plumbing, electricity), doors, windows, even walls.

Since kitchens tend to be positioned at the back of the house, they are often in an ideal situation for extending into the back garden, or knocking through into a corridor or back room to create a more useful space. If you are planning major changes to your kitchen, it is worth finding out how neighbours with the same layout have solved the problem.

One of the first points to consider when reorganizing is the basic floor plan and convenient work triangle mentioned in Chapter 1. There are several tried and tested arrangements of units and appliances which will give an idea of the use you can make of a given shape: The one-wall kitchen, the U-plan kitchen, the L-shaped kitchen and the galley kitchen—for details see page 38. The shape of your room will probably dictate the arrangement.

When you get down to more detailed planning it is useful to know that in a standard European kitchen, base units are 600 mm deep; wall units 300 mm deep; most appliances are 600 mm wide; units come in 300, 500, 600, 1000 or 1200 mm widths, counter tops are usually 900 mm high, with the bottom of wall-hung cabinets 405 mm above that. Even if you are not intending to install ready-made units, their dimensions are ergonomically tested, and they are designed to fit in with standard appliances, so they provide a useful guide if you are building or improvising your own units.

The joy of starting afresh with a large budget shows on the left in marbled counter tops, built-in appliances, plenty of storage, elegant blinds and flooring, and a capacious skylight. Another high budget kitchen, right, with tiled floor, central cook top/eating counter, in clean red and white.

The U-shaped kitchen

This is usually considered the best shape for any kitchen: the triangle idea works well, everything should be within easy reach, and there should be plenty of counter/work space and plenty of storage. It does depend, however, on having a rectangular room.

Still, the U-plan has been proved efficient in both large and small rooms though it's as well to remember that a minimum of 1500 mm (5 ft) and a maximum of 3000 mm (10 ft) is necessary between base cabinets. If your room can take a U-shape and is reasonably large, one side of the U can form a natural dividing line between work and dining space, whether formal or informal. Raise and cantilever part of the counter top on this dividing line and it can act both as a breakfast counter by day, and a barrier against kitchen debris for diners by night.

The L-shaped kitchen

L-shaped kitchens make good dining areas because by locating appliances and cabinets on adjacent walls you create both a compact work space and still have room for a decent-sized dining table. Once again, this sort of arrangement works in a large or in a long narrow kitchen but can waste space in a smaller room where there isn't the same scope for counter and storage space as in a U-shaped plan.

The one-wall kitchen

This is a good idea in a small space, or in a family room or dining room kitchen where the emphasis is more on a general living room than a kitchen. The whole kitchen may be screened off with sliding or folding doors if necessary. Again, it can be useful for a kitchen area off a living room where work and leisure space are divided by a counter or island unit. Unless the wall is very long you do, of course, miss out on storage space unless that is taken care of in other areas.

The corridor or galley kitchen

As its name implies, this can be as neat and effective as a well-organized ship's kitchen–but can also be a disaster if the corridor or galley is open at both ends. When this plan works well it saves a great deal of wear and tear on the cook. However, it will not work for a family or dining/kitchen.

Since space will inevitably be very tight, planning should be as ingenious and imaginative as possible. Slide-out shelves, pull-out work surfaces and storage bins, revolving shelves, pot racks can all be brought into play for maximum effect. For manoeuvrability, there should be at least 1200 mm between the base units on either side. If space does not allow this it might be better to treat it as a one-wall kitchen or an L-shaped kitchen and build in narrow shelves

down the other long wall. You can even use 300 mm deep wall-hung units as base units, surfacing them with a narrow counter top, or you could combine a counter top and stools to make a breakfast bar, with storage space above.

The island kitchen

An island unit in a kitchen (if there is room for one) immediately adds extra work space, storage and interest. It is excellent in a large room which might otherwise lack focus and efficiency but it can also hinder the triangle work flow if the kitchen is not big enough to take it.

The usual function of an island unit is to hold a cook top (which can be self-venting or topped by an extractor hood), closet, shelf and extra work top space, but it can also incorporate an extra small fridge, an extra sink, dishwasher, wine storage, a bar, or an eating counter. If you do not have a cook top and extractor hood, the space above makes an ideal place for a pot or basket rack.

The peninsula kitchen

In a way, this is much the same as an island kitchen except the larger rectangular area is usually used to divide working kitchen space from a family or dining area. Again, you must have enough room for this arrangement but it is a neat way of getting extra storage, breakfast bar, work and buffet space.

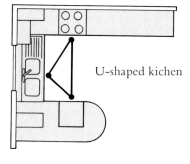

U-shaped kichen

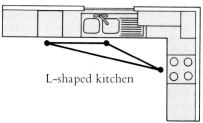

L-shaped kitchen

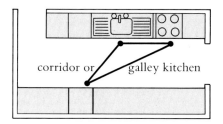

corridor or galley kitchen

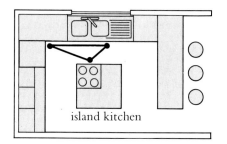

island kitchen

Left: This island unit in an immaculate kitchen-dining room holds dishwasher and sink side by side as well as providing a good counter top/serving space for the table. It also provides a useful focus for the large space. Note how the colours of plants, accessories and food come singing out against the all-white framework, including the stainless steel trim to the table and door.

Above: A one-wall kitchen with a difference—the addition of loud speakers nicely integrated with the back-splash between the units and the pop art displays of groceries. Not a cook's kitchen—more an efficient module for fast food service.

39

Creating a family room

If you are prepared to invest a lot of time and money in your new kitchen you might consider making a sort of kitchen/living or family room; a real 'heart of the home' area, more casual than a living room, more cosy than a working kitchen. If you would like to have this sort of feel but don't think your existing space is big enough, or light enough, or for one reason or another, does not seem to lend itself to such treatment, then consider the surrounding spaces.

What sort of room do you have next door? Is there a scullery for example? Or a lobby of some sort? A sun lounge, verandah or covered porch? A little used dining room or even a corridor or hall? If the walls separating the two are of the partition rather than supporting variety you could take them down and incorporate the space into one much larger room which will make more family sense.

Left and far left: Two different versions of corridor or galley kitchens. Both sides of the space are used for the homely kitchen (far left) which manages to incorporate a desk/eating counter as well as worktops and appliances. The narrower space (left) has made use of an L-shape to avoid too cluttered a look.

Right: An ideal kitchen/dining/living room for an active family.

The kitchen as family room

If a kitchen is big enough it's the obvious place for a general family room. It can do duty as a homework/play area, office and tv room as well as being used in the normal way for preparing, cooking and eating food. Here, a small, slightly awkward alcove to one side of the room has been turned into a useful home office with a typewriter and telephone, although the wall above, with its hanging grid panel for extra pans is still part of the kitchen storage. The large table is just as convenient for writing as for dining. The shelves stretched right across two windows and taking in the wall between make good use of the space to hold tv, cook books and lots of plants and herbs. Pale painted terracotta walls and ceiling are set off by a darker vinyl-tiled floor and plain white tiles above the counter tops are made to look more interesting by being laid on the diagonal. The green and white chair pads are tied on with toning ribbon and there are more green touches in the plants and the light shade. Other interesting features are the industrial serving cart, the spacious industrial shelving and the practical steel rod and hooks running the length of the counter top for utensils.

SPACE AND STYLE

Sometimes, too, it might make sense to turn most of a ground or basement floor into an open-plan kitchen/living/family room/study. As long as you consult the professionals, a surprising number of walls can be taken down with ease and the resulting increase in light and space is clearly amazing.

In a case like this, it might be best to keep most of the kitchen part of the room to one wall and hive it off from the rest of the area with a long island unit which could incorporate extra work and storage space and possibly a cook top, sink and refrigerator as well. A long dividing wall like this would make a good serving unit for every day and a splendid buffet area for a party.

Looking at style

Whatever the shape of your kitchen, it is worth giving some attention to the decoration and accessories to create a distinctive style. The choices are unlimited, but here are some of the characteristic elements which help to give a kitchen a particular atmosphere.

Mediterranean style would be designed to give a cool, smooth working atmosphere, with long slate or marble worktops, terracotta-style tiled floors, and large, walk-in cupboards with thick walls—lined with marble shelves for food storage or racks for pans and crockery.

Roughly plastered walls, shuttered windows and wall-mounted lighting typify this style, with open storage under the worktop and little wall-hung storage. Strings of garlic and bunches of herbs hang from the ceiling, and extra preparation space is provided by a solid table with upright, rush seated chairs around it.

Farmhouse style kitchens are typified by stripped pine, bare brick and perhaps a dresser. Many manufacturers produce pine or pine-effect units, but none will give the easy-on-the-eye, mellow effect that you can get from old pine. Worktops, where they exist, should be in natural materials—wood or tiles. But by using old pieces of furniture of odd shapes and sizes you may well sacrifice the conventional work surface to retain character. A pine or oak refectory table, forming an island unit in the middle of the room, would make up for this. Quarry tyles, brick paviour or wooden boards are typical choices for the floor. For real farmhouse style, you'll need a traditional range (or, more conveniently, an Aga). Back up the cooking facilities of the range with a modern oven, and you'll have all the character with the advantage of modern technology. Go for pretty floral fabrics, patchwork or fresh ginghams, and dot farmhouse chairs and rockers round the room to encourage visitors.

The fresh, country look has evolved over the last few years as people have begun to paint wooden units and replace solid doors with glazed doors to create a lighter atmosphere. Keep to pale colours, even for work surfaces, and choose pale, pretty floral patterns or plain cream for walls and accessories. Coloured tiles or sheet vinyl are ideal for country flooring, or a wooden floor looks equally at home. Use the glazed cupboards to display attractive china and to provide storage space for attractively packaged dry goods.

City slick style can add life to a dull urban kitchen. Go for strong colours and simple geometric patterns. All-white units are cheap, and can be brightened up with coloured tiles and accessories. Or be bold and use more dramatically coloured cupboards. Efficiency is essential in the fast food world of city life, so storage has to be well organized and cleverly designed to leave worktops clear and uncluttered.

Hi-tech is characterized by the use of functional glass and metal. In its extreme form, the domestic Hi-tech kitchen is indistinguishable from a professional kitchen in a good restaurant. Long runs of built-in stainless steel worktop, with hob, sink, chopping board and pastry board built in. Separate cooking areas for different types of food: a pastry chef's corner, a vegetable prepar-

Top right: This kitchen can only be described as not typical (but none the worse for that) with its long sweep of a table incorporating both gas and electric rings and a griddle, its amazing roll-top desk-cum-dresser with its pull-out shelves and enormous storage capacity; its old Raffles Hotel-style rattan long chair and its well stocked wooden shelves.

Bottom right: This is a deliberately Farmhouse-style kitchen. Note all the ingredients: the old pine dresser and well-used refectory table which can also do duty as a preparation area; the capacious old plate rack which holds so much more and drips so much better than a modern version; and the slightly haphazard but practical notion of curtaining the bottom part of the work top rather than filling it in with conventional units. Note too another decorative touch: the frieze of old produce advertisements.

Far right: A highly sophisticated corridor or galley kitchen with the useful addition of one mirrored wall with a small area of floor and wall-hung storage at the end. If these units had been extended all along the now mirrored wall there would hardly have been space to walk the length of the room in comfort. Note how the diagonally-tiled floor, creating an interesting chevron pattern by reflection, gives a further illusion of width and light.

ation area and so on. Cupboards are replaced by open steel shelves, lined with glass storage jars. Flooring is usually synthetic but essentially practical–stud rubber tiles for instance.

Of course, it is possible (even desirable) to draw the best elements of each of these distinctive styles together, to form a perfect, hybrid kitchen, adapted to your needs. They are not to be looked at in isolation and followed to the letter, but if you're not sure about style, they will give you some useful ideas.

These are only some ideas. Many more will be seen in the illustrations and prove that given the will and a bit of imagination you can inject style into almost any space you care to mention.

Left: A good description of this would be cheerful family kitchen designed with ultra-modern Hi-Tech efficiency. The details count: the bright yellow touches in floor border, lamp shade, sofa and accessories; the neat dark blue grid for easy wall attachments; the glass-fronted modular wall units dovetailing in so nicely with the units below and the blue tubular steel for chair frames and sofa legs. The general effect is clean, bright and smart.

Right: Hi-Tech par excellence . . . . with plants and flowers adding just the right sort of contrast.

47

Very few of us can afford all of the appliances we would like all at the same time. What we can do, however, is plan for them. Whether you are designing a kitchen from scratch or updating an old one you must think in terms of priorities, define your most pressing needs, and start from there. Do remember that, contrary to the cynics' view of built-in obsolescence, most major appliances—refrigerators, stoves, dishwashers and so on—are built to last for years, so, as far as possible, you should keep future changes of circumstances in mind as well as your present needs. If your household is likely to expand in any way it might be cheaper in the long run to buy a large model than the more modest affair you had thought of first.

In any case, it is perfectly possible to buy second-hand or re-conditioned models at a fraction of the price of new ones as long as you are prepared to accept the risk that they might eventually develop faults which could prove expensive. Still, they can make good stop-gaps till you can afford new models.

Obviously existing kitchens can be made more efficient with more up-to-date equipment – bigger freezer and/or fridge, a dishwasher,

waste disposal unit and so on—but only if the appliances work hard for you, save time and labour and generally make your particular way of life easier and more enjoyable. A new cooker or whatever can be a tremendous boon and investment but before you go out and spend money ask yourself questions about the way you live: is the pace hectic or leisurely? how many and what sort of meals do you have to provide? are you far from a good supermarket or freezer centre? how much time do you have for shopping? are you out at work all day? do you grow your own vegetables? how often do you entertain? can you spend time on cooking and food preparation or is it always meals in a hurry? The answers will help you decide whether you need say, one vast freezer, or a large one in the garage and a small one in the kitchen, or a microwave plus freezer.

There is plenty of excellent equipment in the kitchen (left), and plenty of room for more to come (an extra fridge or small deep freeze cabinet could be tucked underneath the centre island unit for example). On the right, however, maximum effect is made with the very minimum.

CHOOSING EQUIPMENT

Gas or electricity?

This is really a matter of personal preference and the sort of facilities available in your building (or area – because, of course, nearby gas can be piped in at a cost, or you could use bottled calor gas if you really prefer gas). If you have the possibility of both services in a kitchen, you could opt for a gas cook top and an electric oven; or vice versa; or a mixture of both gas and electric plates to hedge bets should anything go wrong with one or other service, or to take advantage of both sorts of energy for different cooking needs (slow simmering; fast boiling etc.)

Stoves and Ovens

We've come a long way from the free-standing stove with four burners and an oven with maybe a separate grill or broiler. Now you can get models to suit every size, shape and style of kitchen from separate hobs and ovens, to catering-size free-standing models and makes that can be slid or dropped into your work run or counter top for maximum sleekness. Ceramic cook tops can give the semblance of an almost unbroken work surface, and so do the new magnetic induction units that look like tiles, but do not heat up because they use magnetic energy to cook food by energising molecules both in the food and the pan. Both types of cooker top are very smooth in appearance and easy to clean.

Some cook tops combine both gas and electric burners, others have interchangeable parts including a grill, a griddle and a rotisserie. Some tops have built-in deep fryers, and there are stoves with both a conventional and a microwave oven. Some British cooker tops still tend to be niggardly in size and don't make sufficient allowance for four large pans. Other countries seem to manage this better – British manufacturers please copy.

But there are plenty of other refinements to look for: self-cleaning ovens, automatic ignition gas ranges without pilot lights, automatic timers, automatic meat thermometers for perfect roasts, capacious drawer space underneath for plate warming and storing pots and pans, and tops with built-in grills and their own surface-venting systems.

Check the size Most free-standing cookers are 550–600 mm (22–24 ins) deep and extend slightly beyond most cabinets. Standard widths are 510–600 mm (20–24 ins). If you have the space and the cash, you will find that American and some continental cookers are much larger than this. You will be able to choose between a single or a double oven, with an eye-level grill or a grill at waist level, often set into a small top oven. New American models often feature a small, eye-level oven.

Built-in ovens may be designed to

Far left: This particular stove has been neatly dropped into a white wood-trimmed plastic laminate top and is flanked by a pair of pale oak cupboards for pots and pan storage. In fact the whole unit is happily fitted into the alcove left by an old solid fuel kitchen range.

Left: This handsome room with its white hexagonal tiles and interestingly white-stained wood units is extremely well off for cooking power with two full-size wall-mounted ovens and seven burners. With this number of working rings you would certainly need the enormous extractor hood and its inset powerful lighting. There is useful laminated counter space around the cook top and lots of extra cupboards built in underneath. In fact there is as enviable an amount of storage space as there are generous cooking facilities.

Hob design depends to a certain extent on the type of energy used. Top left: This wall-mounted oven and grill has been built into a substantial brick unit and is close to the stainless steel gas hob. Above: Deep set T-shaped shelves, painted a strong blue to contrast with white-tiled walls look bold and dramatic above the ceramic hob set into a butcher-block top. Far left: Gas rings are set into an elegantly green-rimmed top in a brilliantly designed green and white kitchen. The wine racks are stored behind the extractor fan. Left: The tray-like electric cook top here has been neatly fitted into a corner of a small kitchen.

go under the worktop (built-under), either beneath the hob or away from it, or they may fit into housing units so that the oven(s) are more accessible. Built-ins are usually just under 600 mm (24 in) wide, to fit neatly into standard units. Heights vary from about 500 mm (20 in) to 1000 mm (39 in). When you select a model, the literature which comes with it will tell you the exact size of opening and amount of ventilation space you need.

Compact hobs are about 550 × 450 mm (21 × 17 in) but if you have space, go for a large hob to take awkward-sized pans: you don't have to limit yourself to a simple, square configuration – there's no reason why you shouldn't have two or three small hobs in different places.

If you lead a hectically busy life, a microwave oven can be a real life – and time – saver, cooking food in a fraction of the time required by a normal oven. The snag has often been their lack of browning capacity – pale food doesn't look very appealing. But now there are special browning versions that take care of this. And the introduction of a turntable means that food is cooked evenly. Microwaves may be portable (but bulky) counter top models, wall-mounted, or built-in. Their measurements are less than those of standard ovens, although built-in models are the same width as built-in conventional ovens.

Above: Refrigerator and deep freeze are concealed behind wood fascia panels, which tone with the tongue-and-groove of the kitchen units, on either side of a wall-mounted oven in this spacious kitchen/dining room. A dark high level storage unit which matches the table is topped by rattan roller blinds to divide the workmanlike kitchen area from the more elegant dining space.

Left: Another housing unit, this time in white and blue, conceals a well-fitted fridge and freezer. Note how units have been cleverly fitted all around the small window.

Refrigerators and Freezers

The model of refrigerator and freezer you choose should depend on the size—or potential size—of your family and your work and cooking habits. Generally speaking, a 140 litre (5 cubic feet) refrigerator and 140–170 litres (5–6 cubic feet) of freezer space is ample for a couple and you should add another cubic foot per person in your household. If you can shop only once a week for example, you will need much more deep freeze space than if you can shop every day. If you cannot have a separate freezer you should look at a refrigerator with maximum freezer space and capacious food storage compartments. A good many of the latest models have sealed meat and vegetable drawers with adjustable temperature and humidity control to keep food fresher for longer.

Obviously frost-free models which mean you never have to defrost are as useful as self-cleaning ovens, and additional luxuries include iced water and crushed ice dispensers, automatic ice makers *and* the kind of American model with almost instant (that is to say about an hour) automatic ice cream and sorbet or sherbert-makers.

Separate deep freezers come in chest or upright models and are ideal for people with large gardens and plenty of produce to store and also for stashing away bulk buys and supermarket bargains.

Dishwashers

Really good dishwashers will clean everything from fine china and glass to encrusted saucepans and casseroles with settings that range from gentle wash to super scrub cycles. If you are a small family, look for models with the sort of controls that allow you rinse-and-hold cycles—a short cycle which rinses dishes for a short time to get rid of dried-on food and any smells so that they can then wait till you have a full load to put through. If you are a large family, or cook a lot, you should definitely look for a machine with a scrub cycle so you are not always hand-scouring pots and pans. Look too, for models with the sort of shelving that allows you to programme the machine to start work hours later and will make the operation a whole lot quieter, and the kinds that have soft food disposal units to prevent blocked drains.

If you do not have space for a build-in model beside or under the sink, there are portables available on wheels so that they can be rolled to the table for loading and back to the sink where they can be connected to the taps and drains for washing. Some have butcher-block tops so that they can double as extra work tops. If you move and have more space, many portables are convertible and can be built-in.

Most models are 60 cm (24 in) wide to fit in with average counter top measurements.

Fitting in the equipment

This is a good-sized working kitchen which has to accommodate a wealth of laundry as well as cooking equipment and make room for all the extra appliances essential to modern living. The most sensible way to arrange them all within the given space is to use the U-shaped layout, perfectly possible here because the room has the required width to make it work. One end of the room has windows at each corner and these make it easy to divide the space fairly naturally into two reasonably separate areas. Corner sinks make it possible to provide one area for clothes washing and another for dishes and vegetable preparation. The left-hand side of the kitchen takes the washing and drying machines, fridge, deep freeze and a desk unit with a shelf above it for a small home computer. This is used for keeping accounts, recipes and vital household information. The right-hand run includes dishwasher, drawer and cupboard storage and double oven and microwave. A centre island unit incorporates a cook top with both grill and electric hob and extra work surface. Wall units on both sides provide plenty of general storage. The whole room is given a fresh light look with yellow and white ceramic tiles, white lozenge-shaped floor tiles, white units and wooden Venetian blinds.

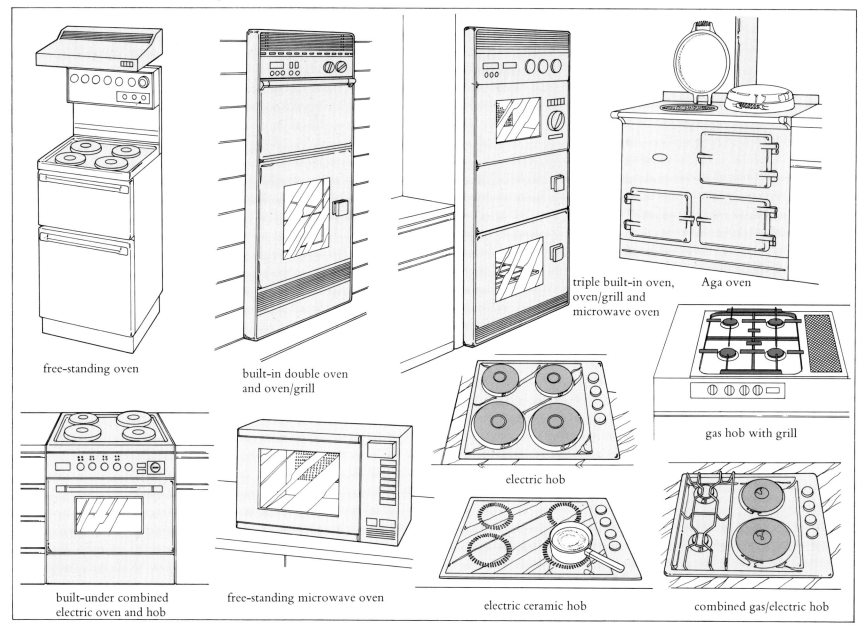

free-standing oven

built-in double oven
and oven/grill

triple built-in oven,
oven/grill and
microwave oven

Aga oven

gas hob with grill

electric hob

built-under combined
electric oven and hob

free-standing microwave oven

electric ceramic hob

combined gas/electric hob

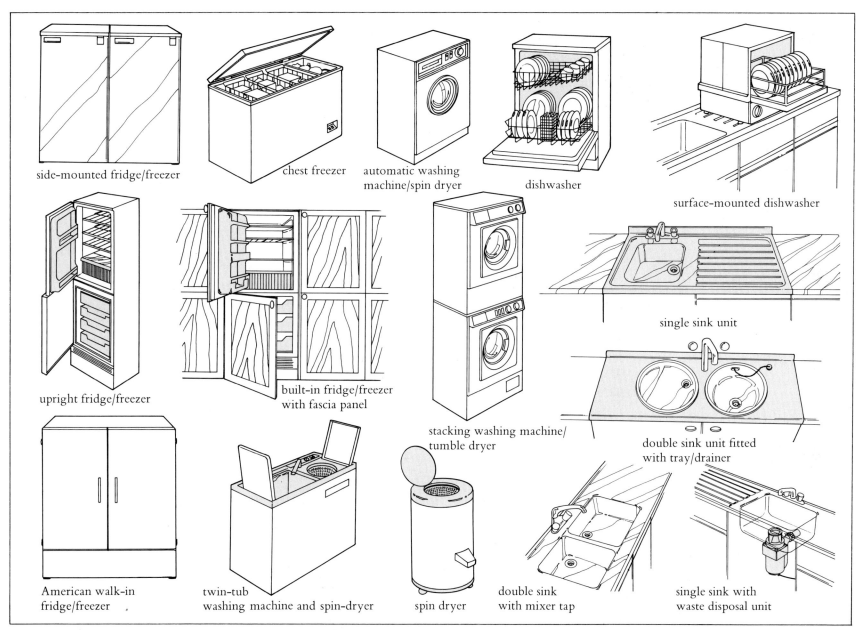

side-mounted fridge/freezer

chest freezer

automatic washing machine/spin dryer

dishwasher

surface-mounted dishwasher

upright fridge/freezer

built-in fridge/freezer with fascia panel

stacking washing machine/ tumble dryer

single sink unit

double sink unit fitted with tray/drainer

American walk-in fridge/freezer

twin-tub washing machine and spin-dryer

spin dryer

double sink with mixer tap

single sink with waste disposal unit

CHOOSING EQUIPMENT

Top: Washing machine and tumble dryer are set below oven and refrigerator and are flanked by a ceramic hob in this display of appliances.

Above, left and right: The same pair of sinks, set into a tiled worktop, has
been photographed twice to show its versatility. The rounded sink on the left is fitted with a drainer in one and with a wooden chopping block top, complete with cut-out for rinsing, in the other which has the effect of increasing the work space.

Sinks

If you have the space (and the money) it is useful to have two and even three sinks: one for soaking dishes, one for preparing vegetables and one smaller one for a waste or garbage disposer. A waste disposer can, of course, be fitted into a single main sink, but do make sure your building or house has the sort of drainage system that will not be fouled up by liquid refuse in bulk. Some sinks come complete with extra wood cutting board surface to fit across the top when necessary and so provide extra work space; others have small spray attachments at the side to aid cleaning. If you are short of space do not forget the inch-saving corner varieties.

The most common choice for taps is a single swing spout with either one or two handles. Materials are generally stainless steel, porcelain-covered cast iron, or the new Corian, the marble-like plastic which makes a neat and effective all-in-one counter and sink.

Waste disposers and rubbish (trash) compactors

The newest waste disposers can handle up to 1 litre (2 pints) of waste food at a time very much more quickly than the old bone-chilling (and bone-crunching) models. Rubbish or trash compactors can squash up cardboard boxes, cartons, tins, cans and bottles to a quarter of

their original size. They may be worth considering if you live in a high-rise flat, or have infrequent refuse collection, but they do take up space. They can be located almost anywhere in the kitchen and attach-ed to the same sort of outlet as an electric stove.

Cooker hoods

Although some stoves have built-in self-venting outlets, there is an en-ormous market for hoods of every description and style with built-in fans for ventilation and to remove cooking smells. Most units need to be on an outside wall or ducted to vent outdoors but others can be bought which are ventless, recircu-lating the air through activated char-coal filters which should be changed regularly.

All of them have incorporated light bulbs to give extra light over the work top.

Washing machines and dryers

If there is any possibility of placing washing machines and dryers away from the kitchen you should con-sider it. Detergents and dirty clothes don't mix very well with food preparation and in any case the most sensible place to position both appli-ances is somewhere near the bedroom/bath area. Standard mach-ines measure 600 mm ($23\frac{5}{8}$ in) deep by 595 mm ($23\frac{3}{8}$ in) wide, to fit between units and can be stacked one above the other. But, unless you have a separate utility room, that does not leave much space nearby for storing laundry supplies and accessories or setting down the just-cleaned laundry. If there is room for a 1300 mm (5 ft) cupboard or closet just outside the kitchen, bedroom or bathroom, say in a corridor, or lobby, this would be a better solution. It would give room for a washer and dryer to stand side by side under a convenient counter top. Better still, if there is room, would be a 2500 mm (8 ft) wide louvre-fronted closet which would give you space for washing machine, dryer, clothes hamper and general purpose cabinet with a metre wide (3 ft) double door wall cabinet above and a clothes rod to hang out just dried permanent press clothing. The units could have a counter top and there would need to be efficient lighting.

If you really cannot find the space anywhere else in the home you will have to try to squeeze space in the kitchen (or go to a launderette). It would be best to install the appliances side by side in order to keep worktop continuity, and do not forget that most dryers need to be vented to an outside wall.

Appliances and units alike in this modern kitchen/dining room are all fronted by an interesting closed louvre finish which resembles an updated version of the old roll-topped desks.

CHOOSING EQUIPMENT

glass-fronted cabinets become
decoration in their own right

spotlight over cooking area
with blue-grey shade

stove flue enamelled
blue to match Aga

blue-grey painted
frames tone
with stove

blue and white
accessories
all add to the
general effect

refrigerator
concealed
behind aerated
cupboard door

two corner doors
open together
on hinge for
easy access

well-designed and generous
drawer and cupboard space
enables only good stuff
to be displayed

*This charming blue-grey and cream
kitchen combines the appeal and
solidity of traditional fittings with the
convenience of modern appliances.
The stove-enamelled Aga cooker is
gas-powered for ease of use. The base
units both conceal items like the
refrigerator and provide sufficient
storage to enable only the more elegant
objects to be stored in the glass-fronted
cupboards (inset) with their clever
slotted shelves.*

slots cut in
shelves to
hold plates

Kitchen units and cabinets

If you are handy yourself, can employ a good carpenter, or go to a custom cabinet maker, you can make or obtain literally any size or type of unit to fit the most awkward spaces. Another ploy is to buy unfinished or whitewood cabinets and fit them into your space, finishing them off yourself with paint or stain.

If you are going for a fully fitted kitchen, you will find the units are made up of three elements: the carcass (basic cupboard and shelves), the doors and drawer fronts, and the work surface which runs along the top. Usually, all can be bought separately. In some ranges, you can buy decor panels to fit the front of specially designed built-in appliances, making them match the cupboards.

Ready made cabinets come in a huge choice of finishes, colours, and measurements. Heights for wall cabinets range from 300 mm (12 in) – good for the space over a refrigerator – to 1000 mm (39 in). The depth from wall to face is a standard 300 mm (12 in) and widths run from 230 mm (9 in) to 600 mm (24 in) for single door cabinets to 1000 mm (39 in) to 1200 mm (48 in) for double door models. Corner cabinets with a single door and either fixed or revolving shelves can be mounted diagonally across a corner to use every inch of available space.

Base units generally stand 900 mm (36 in) from the floor if you count the worktop as well and widths match the wall hung cabinets, though the depth is generally twice as much. You can buy them with doors, drawers, or both, and with different depths for different drawers. Again, there are many refinements to choose from: glide-out vegetable storage equipment, wine racks, slide-out chopping blocks, bottle drawers, silver storage drawers, pot lid holders, tray storage, sliding trays for linens and cutlery racks. Alternatively, you can buy standard but empty units and fill them with your own choice of such 'organizers' from other sources.

Pantry or food storage cabinets are specially made to accommodate cans and dry goods (breakfast cereals, jams, flour and other packaged goods). Often they are heavily hinged with one can deep shelving from top to bottom of the doors for maximum use of space. You can buy them in wall, floor or full length sizes.

Utility or broom cupboards are generally 300 mm (12 in) or 600 mm (24 in) deep, 1950 mm (7 ft) tall and from 500 mm (22 in) to 600 mm (24 in) wide. They consist of one tall space with an upper shelf for brooms, vacuum cleaners, mops and cleaning supplies. Similarly-shaped cabinets can be bought as housing units for particular models of wall oven and for refrigerators.

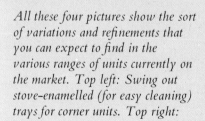

All these four pictures show the sort of variations and refinements that you can expect to find in the various ranges of units currently on the market. Top left: Swing out stove-enamelled (for easy cleaning) trays for corner units. Top right:

Open-shelved corner unit – ideal for better-looking possessions. Bottom left: Pull-out trash container drawer which neatly holds rubbish bin. Bottom right: Deep drawers have aerated wire racks for saucepans and their lids.

The central fact to acknowledge about any sort of storage is that there is rarely enough of it, and this is certainly true in the kitchen.

Be ruthless

The kitchen is the one room where you should literally use every inch, nook, cranny, piece of ceiling, window, door or side of cabinet; in fact the key to successful and efficient kitchen storage is to use every possible surface, and to assemble equipment and accessories by the places where they are the most needed. Start your kitchen re-organization with a drastic sort-out and throw-out. Don't weaken. If you do not use an object once a day, or at least once a week, it does not deserve prime storage space (that is within easy reach and somewhere between knee and eye level). Put it instead at the back of a base cabinet or high up on a wall cabinet, or in the space, if there is one, between wall cabinets and ceiling which you can always turn into a second tier of cabinets by adding fronts to match your other units. Things which are used once or twice a year—turkey roasting pans, huge party casseroles, picnic baskets, should be rigorously stashed right away, if possible out of the kitchen

altogether—under the stairs, in an attic, in the basement or garage in a house; in some more remote cupboard in a flat or apartment. And what about all those gadgets lying loose in drawers? Would they be tidier and more accessible hung on pegboards?

If you have not used something for literally years the chances are that it won't come in useful for a rainy day (the hoarder's excuse) and that you probably won't *ever* use it. So give it away, send it to a jumble sale, sell it if you can, or just throw it away. Whatever you do, be tough . . . Don't keep it. If you do, it will almost certainly be the beginning of the end and you will never get properly organized. Perhaps one should keep a picture of hideous confusion pinned to the kitchen door in the same way as slimmers keep a fat photo taped to the fridge as a deterrent to snacking.

Lovely storage for the tidy-minded (left), it could become a mess for anyone else. Still, the open shelves make life easy for the organized cook and the pull-out wire baskets are a good idea for fruit and vegetables. If you are not so tidy the kitchen on the right is a better bet.

Far left: A clever pull-out unit the full height of the run of cabinets makes day-to-day necessities clearly visible and easily accessible.

Above: Two wood plate drainers flank the window here to provide excellent storage. A shelf across the window connects the racks and gives further storage space. A wooden rod suspended from the ceiling holds yet more equipment.

Left: Even the space between these handsome units has been used for storage.

Right: The staggered top cupboards of these good-looking units allow more wall space for hanging equipment that is decorative and functional.

Be logical

This simply means that instead of bending and scuffling around for saucepans stacked up in a dark base unit, try hanging them from hooks near the sink (where you are going to fill them with water) or near the stove. Keep herbs and spices on small racks just above or by the cook top. Store pulses, rice, pasta, sugar, flour and condiments by the worktop or preparation area. Stash old plastic or paper shopping bags near the rubbish or garbage bin and then you can re-cycle them as bin liners. Everyday plates can be stored upright in a wooden plate rack above the dishwasher or by the sink. This is much easier than keeping them in piles in a cupboard or closet. Similarly, mugs and cups used regularly can be kept on hooks near the stove top, and glasses can be kept in a cabinet near the washing machine. Store wooden spoons, whisks, colanders, sieves in containers or from hooks by the worktop or cooker top, wherever you need them most, and keep oil, vinegars, condiments, herbs and garlic near salad bowls.

Be ingenious

Once you have thoroughly reorganized your existing storage you can look around for new surfaces to conquer. Bunches of herbs and pot and saucepan racks can be hung from the ceiling. You can fix tiny narrow shelves or racks to the inside of cabinet doors; attach spice racks, hooks, more shelves (to take cook books?) to the sides of cabinets; add further shelves just above worktops on the splashback areas, and add shallow shelves 300–450 mm (12–18 in) above cook tops and sinks with hooks attached to the edges for various bits of equipment such as measuring jugs and ladles.

As usual in most rooms, corners are often a wasted area. You might be able to build a corner unit across the angle of two worktops for cook books, or more spices and condiments, with more storage space for jars on top. If there is not room for this you might utilize the space by making slots in the counter top to take your cooking knives, or you could suspend them from a magnetic bar just above out of reach of children. Think too, about using the underside of your cabinets for kitchen paper holders, more suspended spice racks, or for hooks to hang just about anything.

Spare bits of wall which are too small for conventional cabinets can be used for mounting peg boards for small implements and utensils; or pin-board for recipes, bills, receipts, reminders to the family and to yourself. Make better use of your base cabinets by fixing slide-out towel racks to the doors, and by installing swivel storage shelves to do away with all that groping around for things at the back. Shallow alcoves can be used for yet more narrow shelves just the depth of one can or bottle or for mounting a magnetic knife-rack; awkward spaces, say between stove and storage cabinets, can be used for trays.

Eating in the kitchen

This kitchen–dining room is first and foremost a good working kitchen which happens to have space to fit in table and chairs. Neatly checked and sprigged wallpaper is teamed with cream tiles which have thin blue grouting between them. This has the effect of giving continuity of colour and pattern to the background. The cream paintwork and cream Holland roller blinds at the window keep to the theme. The floor is deeper and warmer with ochre bricks. The wood-framed kitchen units have dark blue laminate panels and the same blue is repeated in accessories like the kettle. The cooker top set in the island unit, which makes a useful serving area for the dining table, is surrounded with more cream tiles and the blue and cream scheme is carried right through to the hanging light over the dining table. Track lighting in the centre of the ceiling provides good overall illumination and strip lights are recessed under the top units by the window. For all its neat simplicity it's a cheerful kitchen. The rounded curves of the wood table and chairs add a homely relaxed note to all the clean straight lines of the room.

ORGANIZED STORAGE

Right: The pull-out work table in the middle of this cheerful kitchen divides cooking and workroom space as well as providing an excellent sewing/writing surface with telephone conveniently to hand. Such bonus workspace means that one can take advantage of lulls in the middle of cooking and preparation to get on with other jobs—or catch up with bills, lists and letters and still keep an eye on the meal. After all, the table could just as well hold a typewriter, or drawing materials or any other working equipment.

Far right: A counter top has been extended here to take a typewriter, filing tray and a good worklight with again a telephone at arm's length. Of course, the same space can equally well be used as a serving area for the table.

A place for paperwork

It is useful to have some sort of desk where you can write lists, pay bills, file receipts, copy recipes, and take messages. Again there might be some odd space between units that you could span to make a desk top, or you might add a swing-up flap at the end of a worktop which can be raised and lowered as required. Another alternative is to widen or deepen a counter top so that you can sit at it with a stool; or you can convert a drawer to a small work counter/worktop/cutting board by fitting a block of wood on top which you can draw out and sit at..

Think about the benefits of a kitchen telephone installed on or near the improvised desk top within, if possible, easy reach of the stove. It is infuriating to have to run and answer the telephone in the middle of some intricate sauce or dish. To have a phone within arm's length of the cook top makes a world of difference to your general convenience so see that any phone has a long extension cord.

Such comparatively slight and inexpensive changes can make an enormous improvement to the way your kitchen works, by reducing the amount of to-ing and fro-ing and getting rid of many possible sources of irritation, inconvenience and interruption. After all, the less hassle enjoy being the more you'll there.

Making a pin-board

One of the simplest ways to make a pin-board is to buy a cork bath mat and mount it on the wall. For a more substantial board, fix unsealed cork tiles to the wall, and surround them with beading or picture framing (architraving to

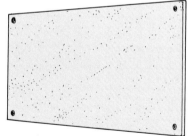

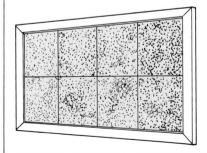

match your door surrounds is a neat solution), mitring the corners for a neat finish.

For a fabric-covered board, use coloured felt to cover a piece of softboard, wrapping excess fabric over the edges and glueing it to the back. Mount the board on the wall, using round-headed screws.

Only when you have made your plans, decided on your work sequence, bought your appliances and thought about the style of room you would like to create, can you focus on the treatment of the rest: the framework of walls, floor, window and ceiling as well as the sort of tiles, splashback and worktop you would like. This, of course, is the actual decoration of the room, the process which comes first in most areas, but certainly last in the kitchen planning sequence. Last, but *never* least: colours, surfaces and embellishments have their own particular and important role to play in kitchen comfort.

Walls

By the time you have put up an appropriate amount of cabinets and storage there is not usually much wall left to cover. It is often possible to tile a large proportion of the wall for guaranteed ease of maintenance. Paint, however, should always be washable – do not use emulsion because you will not be able to wash grease and smoke off easily, but rather use gloss or eggshell finishes.

White or earth colours – tobaccos, umbers, sand, sludgy green, pine green – are particularly appropriate with food, while blue and white, green and white, red or pink and white and a sunny chrome yellow, always look good and fresh. Try painting walls white and colouring woodwork, or vice versa. It depends very much on the units you choose. Obviously, if they are a colour as opposed to white or wood, you should choose a background that blends with them.

If you decide on a wallpaper, try to use a paper-backed vinyl, a vinyl impregnated fabric paper, or a PVC wallcovering. Or else paint the surface of ordinary paper with a coat or two of eggshell or gloss polyurethane for a practical protective finish.

Stripped or new brick makes a good kitchen background, so does tongue-and-groove wood panelling or panelling of wide wooden planks. Bricks should be sealed with a masonry stabiliser, while wood should be waxed, varnished or painted.

The units are in place, the floor is stripped, sanded and polished and there is still plenty of scope and general living space to play with in this large loft, left. Very positive decorating decisions in this kitchen, right; co-ordinating red and white fabric and paper everywhere.

shelf unit suspended
from ceiling provides
additional storage

glossy red diagonal
tongue-and-groove
boarding adds space

charcoal-filter
extractor hood

light
positioned
over work
area

*The warm and cheerful
look of this small kitchen
has been achieved with a
fairly low outlay.
Tongue-and-groove
boarding set on the
diagonal has been given a
coating of brilliant red
paint. The suspended shelf
over the worktop holds
plants and spices and also
supports a charcoal
extractor hood.*

double sink
unit with
drainer rack
fitting

mosaic-
tiled work
surface

curtains conceal
food and utensils

If you have a kitchen/dining room and want to make it look particularly warm and comfortable you could make a visual division between working and eating areas by stapling the dining walls with a cheap cotton and then spraying on Scotchgard. Again, you could give your room an interesting old country look by adding a 'wainscot' of boarding to a free wall, or at least some moulding at dado level.

Ceilings

Unless you have a particular pretty beamed or coved ceiling it is often a good idea to lower the ceiling area in a kitchen. This enables you to put in recessed lighting, or to add an acoustic or tongue-and-groove wood finish. Acoustic tiles are used for ceilings rather than walls and are made to absorb sound. They have to be suspended from battens and are most often made from pre-finished, slotted insulation board, polystyrene or fibreglass. Tongue-and-groove pine boarding looks good; it should be sealed with polyurethane to protect the wood and needs hardly any maintenance—just wiping over occasionally. In America, the virtues of the old pressed metal ceilings have been rediscovered and redeployed. But if you do not want to add a ceiling covering, simply paint the surface with white, or very pale emulsion to reflect as much light as possible.

Left: The glass roof to the ceiling of this kitchen lets light flood in but keeps heat out. It has been fitted with a stretched, diagonally-striped green and white roller blind which gives good protection and also looks cool and decorative. The all-cream units and walls blend with the tiled floor and provide an excellent background colour for the intense green of the plants which underline the greenhouse feel, as do the vertical louvered blinds.

Above: Mini-print hexagonal tiles and floor tiles that match in shape if not colour, are nicely offset by the strawberry print curtains in this wood-trimmed, friendly little kitchen.

Floors

Kitchen floors need to be tough enough to withstand all sorts of spills, grease and damp, comfortable enough to stand on for long periods, and handsome to look at. The choice of covering in fact, very much depends on the sort of style you have set yourself. If you want a rustic kitchen, then quarry, brick or Mexican or French terracotta tiles look very splendid. Slate is marvellous to look at but at a marvellous price, and there is an enormous choice in ceramic tiles which can be mixed in among the terracottas for an ethnic Mexican or Provencale, Italian, Spanish or Portuguese look. Terracotta tiles, brick, flagstone, slate, terrazzo and non-slip ceramic are all durable, impressive, good to look at and easy to clean. They generally come in a range of beautiful colours and pleasing shapes. Most are heavy and therefore only suitable for laying at ground-floor level or where floors are exceptionally strong. All

Left: A bright cheerful kitchen where vivid colours are carefully balanced. Red/white/yellow checked vinyl flooring co-ordinates the red and white checked tiles and red stripes with the yellow in the accessories.

Right: Brick-shaped terracotta tiles have a country look to them and nicely bridge the gap between rusticity and modernity in this pleasant kitchen.

Sensible surfaces

Kitchen, floor, walls, counter tops, table, units and windows all need covering in as practical and harmonious a way as possible. Choosing the appropriate materials for all these various surfaces requires careful budgeting as well as serious thought since they have to look good, wear well and be just right for their particular purpose. In this predominantly blue and white room the major investment was in the long run of Corian counter top and sink. French blue and white ceramic tiles look fresh and pretty and their cost is reasonable considering how durable and maintenance free they are. The blue and white floor tiles are vinyl—easy on the feet and easy to keep clean. Here they have been cut into interesting patterns. The blue and white theme is taken up again at the window where the cotton blinds are white with a vertical blue stripe and their pelmets are dark blue with horizontal white stripe, all given Scotchgard treatment. The same dark blue fabric is used for the seat cushions, tied with blue tape. Table, chairs and louvre door units are all in the same handsome mellow pine.

of these treatments are as hard on the feet as they are easy on the eye – but sometimes, as I have said, good appearances win over practical considerations. If both price and hardness bother you, there are acceptable alternatives in vinyl, and cork coated with vinyl which can look very good too. Both vinyl – in sheet or tile form – and vinyl-coated cork are easy to maintain.

Hi-Tech and more sleekly designed kitchens look good with white tiled floors whether ceramic or vinyl, but again you could use cork and vinyl, or composition tiles or even linoleum which has taken on a new lease of life now that people have realised how well it can look inserted with other colours.

Wood treated with polyurethane to withstand spills and grease can look very handsome, especially in a dining kitchen, and old floors can be spruced up with paint, various painted finishes and stencilling, protected with extra coats of varnish.

When choosing flooring for a kitchen/diner, make sure the surface is suitable for both functions, or delineate one area from another by using different types of flooring. For example, if you have quarry tiles in the kitchen, they may be rather cold on the feet for dinner guests lingering over coffee, as well as being noisy when chairs scrape across them. You may find that people are encouraged to use the room as more of a gathering place if the floor of the dining area is covered with colourful rugs, and even with vinyl flooring

Above left: Polyurethaned wood boards are a handsome contrast to this mainly white kitchen with its distinctive blue and white tiled border. Note the repetition of the boarding on the ceiling – here painted white – and the linear effect of the blinds.

Above right: Graduated hexagonal tiles look quietly handsome against white units and butcher-block tops. For the accident prone, vinyl tiles simulated to look like earthenware tiles might be better.

Emphatic flooring. Top left: Brilliant blocks of primary colours set into black make imaginative use of composition tiles. The bold colours are picked up again in the flowers and also repeated in the accessories. Above: Gleaming ceramic tiles cover floor, counter tops and walls in a kitchen planned to last. Far left: Neat herringbone parquet makes a warm-looking expanse in an otherwise fairly austere kitchen. Left: Both ceiling and floor have been painted a stunning red in this compact kitchen.

SUITABLE SURFACES

you can create a change of atmosphere around the table by changing the colour of the floor or simply by adding a rug.

Windows

There is no point at all in elaborate window coverings in the kitchen. They only get dirty, greasy and in the way. It is far better to use café curtains, short, tied-back curtains, or blinds. Fabric should be easily washed or cleaned cotton, or vinylised cotton (for roller blinds). Otherwise use Venetian blinds in plastic or wood which can be easily wiped, or wooden shutters, or no covering at all. Shelves look good and are practical across a window and can be made of glass, or wood, or metal grid for a Hi-Tech look. Alternatively, just hang plants from hooks above the window, or stand small pots of plants along the windowsill, making sure that the ones you select are going to be happy with the kind of light, temperature and humidity you are providing. Used this way, with massed greenery, or collections of glass on glass shelves, the kitchen window becomes a strong focal point.

If your kitchen has a whole wall of window, this needn't be a problem. Either treat it as a feature in its own right, with a striking blind or shutters; give it as much impact as possible and let the view and the light pour in. Or, if you think it steals

too much potential storage space you could consider sacrificing some of it. If you're desparate for storage space it's often possible to build units right around a window so that the window acquires a recessed effect and becomes an essential part of the arrangement. In this case, the simpler the window treatment the better; plain blinds, café curtains or just left bare.

Worktops

Worktops have to be as durable as floors, able to withstand chopping, hot utensils and spills, and still be good to look at. Formica or plastic laminate is very popular but you must be careful not to chop directly on to it (use a chopping board) or to put down hot pots and saucepans. Once ruined it is extremely difficult to put right.

Ceramic tiles—which can be continued up the space between counter top and unit to make a handsome splashback—come in a huge range of colours and designs and can look spectacular, gentle or fresh depending on the effect you want. However, the grouting can easily get discoloured and dirty-looking, so it might be better to start off with a dark grouting from the beginning. Also, you should be wary of putting down pots and pans straight from the stove; this might cause the ceramic to crack.

Butcher-block and wood counter

Left: This terracotta-tile effect vinyl floor is almost indistinguishable from the real thing and makes a smart contrast to the white tiled units and brilliant yellows and greens of the rest of the kitchen/dining room.

Above: The red sink fits neatly into the white-tiled counter top and blends with the dotted wallpaper.

Right: The Corian counter top used here with its moulded integral sinks and generous depth, not only looks good with its marble appearance but could hardly be more practical. It is hardwearing and relatively stain-resistant. Damage, like scratches, can be removed with reasonable ease.

SUITABLE SURFACES

tops are sturdy and look good but they are not very practical near the sink surrounds or anywhere where there is water because they can warp and the grain can rise up. If you are using wood as a continuous work surface, introduce some variety; let in a square of marble or ceramic tile for making pastry; surround your sink with stainless steel, tile or plastic laminate rather than wood, which tends to lift up and warp.

Corian is a mineral-filled plastic that feels like marble but is immensely more practical. This material is ideal for countertops and pastry surfaces since it is very durable, resistant to most stains, and does not burn or warp. It comes in white, cream and a slightly veined beige. It may be cut and glued to give a virtually seamless surface.

For more ideas on renewing or replacing worktops, see Chapter 2.

Splashbacks
These can be made of plastic laminate, Corian or ceramic tile, which is still the most popular. They can be plain, patterned or flowered, bevelled, or a mixture. Tiles can be laid on the diagonal or in a basket weave design to produce handsome effects.

A calm, pretty pink and white kitchen. The laminate top to match the units beneath, contrasts happily with the pink tiles, painted ceiling and ceiling-mounted spots.

Safety rules

Statistics reveal the horrifying truth that there are more accidents in the home than on the road and that most of these take place in the kitchen and to children. So safety should be a priority, whether starting from scratch, or just re-vamping.

To avoid all possible causes of accidents take the following precautions:

Always unplug small appliances when they are not in use, and don't let appliance cords dangle over the edge of counters where they can be reached by children. Keep flexes as short as is convenient to avoid a spaghetti of cables.

Choose non-slip flooring and always mop up spills immediately.

Treat food processor blades with the greatest respect. Handle them gingerly; wash them carefully; don't ever leave them soaking, submerged in water in case someone else unsuspectingly puts their hand in. They can be lethal. Equally, if they are in the dishwasher, pick them out very carefully.

Whenever possible, cook on the back burners of cook tops or stoves, especially when children are around. Make sure pot handles are turned towards the back of the stove and that the oven door is firmly closed.

If you have small children around cover electric outlets with safety caps or tape.

Never pull any appliance–kettle, mixer–out of its socket without switching off first.

Never add dishwasher detergent (which is toxic) until the last moment, then close door immediately. Make sure that dishwasher doors are always latched tight. Left down they are a temptation to children who might climb onto them and tip the whole appliance.

Place all poisonous, potentially poisonous and toxic household cleaners, detergents and scourers on the highest possible shelf. Never keep any of these in innocent looking old lemonade bottles particularly if the original labels are still on.

Keep all trash and garbage out of children's reach and place any old container which held a toxic substance into the outside dustbin or garbage can as soon as it is finished.

Don't ever leave your children alone in the kitchen; they have even been known to get trapped inside fridges and freezers.

Never leave an iron on if you leave the room, and never let young children near an ironing board while you are ironing.

When you are serving up hot dishes make sure that toddlers and young children are well out of the way.

Keep sharp knives well out of the reach of children–either on a magnetic panel set back and above the worktop; in slots made at the back of the worktop, or in a knife block set well back too.

Try not to use long tablecloths, or at least tablecloths within the reach of a yank from small hands.

If you have high shelves keep a proper, solid stepladder within easy reach and do not climb on chairs or worktops.

Always keep a first aid and burn treatment kit in the kitchen, near the stove, ready for emergencies.

If you possibly can, keep a small fire extinguisher to hand near the stove and make sure that everyone knows how to use it. It's too late to absorb the instructions when the kitchen is in flames. Ensure it is suitable for fat fires and electric fires. A fire blanket, hung to one side of the cooker, may also be useful, as long as you understand how to use it.

Do not keep any fabrics near the stove or cook top: if the window is near the stove top do not use curtains. Nor should you keep drying up cloths or oven gloves in the sort of position where they could drop or drag on a burner.

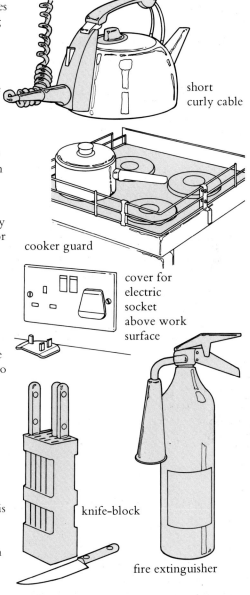

short curly cable

cooker guard

cover for electric socket above work surface

knife-block

fire extinguisher

Cooking and eating go together, so naturally the next step is to decide where and in what sort of style you are going to serve and eat meals. It really hardly matters if this happens in a room of its own, in the kitchen, the living room, or even the hall. Dining rooms today, are wherever the food is served.

If you do have a separate dining room, you're lucky. It need contain no more than a sideboard, table and chairs and can be decorated in its own individual way. If you do a great deal of formal or business entertaining then this sort of dining room is essential. But these days, with space at a premium, a room kept solely for dining is rare; the chances are that it has to double as a work room, say for hobbies like model making, or as a quiet place where the family can get on with homework, studying or other paperwork. And far more likely is the dining room which is no more than a corner of another room. This, of course, makes it simple to furnish; all you really need are a table and chairs which fit in well with the rest of the room. A kitchen-dining room is ideal for a family; its cosy, convenient and economical since it saves heating another room. In tiny flats

and bed-sitters it's more often the living room that has to make space for dining, in which case it's a good idea to separate the two functions with either a physical division—like an arch, trellis or shelving—or with visual treatment like different lighting or flooring, or perhaps a change of colour or mood.

But whatever your dining area consists of, organizing it, giving it character and interest can be challenging and stimulating. In fact, the dining room should be a particularly interesting room to decorate, because, like the bathroom, it is generally used for comparatively short periods at a time, and then mostly at night. As long as its main purpose is borne in mind—that of providing a relaxed, comfortable and enjoyable area for eating which is also a good background for the food that is served—it can,

The clean-lined dining area in this white-tiled kitchen left, is neatly separated from the work part by handsome structural columns. The clever updated chandelier effect is achieved by hooking up five green and white lights to one outlet. The summery dining area, right, is divided from the work area by kitchen units.

WHERE TO EAT

theoretically, be as inventive, curious, and as experimental as you like.

Before you embark on the decoration, however, you need to have the practical considerations firmly in mind. Decide exactly what functions the room has to fulfil. Ask yourself these questions:

● How many people will eat in the dining room regularly?

● What is the maximum number of diners which will have to be accommodated at a sit-down meal?

● How much storage space is necessary for china and cutlery; for dining accessories; for other items not related to eating – books, papers, sewing equipment and so on?

● Is the room the only dining space or are family meals usually taken elsewhere?

● Will it be used mainly at night, or does it need to look fresh for breakfast, serviceable for lunch and intimate for dinner parties?

● Are your needs likely to change over the next few years – will you have children to cope with; are you likely to entertain more often than you do at present?

Would a very bold, outrageous, or dramatic look be too overwhelming in a dining room which all the family are going to want to use at different times? I remember an all-black room I saw years ago which has always stuck in my mind: black velvet walls, black carpet, ebony table and chairs, black lacquer side table. The only relief was in the tablecloth, napkins, china and flowers which varied from spanking white, to black and white, to brilliant yellow or green. The lighting was subtle: concealed behind pelmets, inset into the ceiling, bounced up from uplights on the floor, flickering from candles. And the room always looked beautiful, except on a gloomy winter's day, when it was frightful. Such rooms are definitely not for breakfast.

Another room I remember for its verve was all shiny dark green lacquered walls, gilded carpet and *trompe l'oeil* painted walls which looked like real draperies: a theatrical, stunning experience. But the fact that so few rooms stand out in my memory is not so surprising. On the whole, dining rooms fall into pretty familiar categories, furnished with pretty familiar types of furniture, colours and accessories, And perhaps that is as it should be. The serious diner likes to feel comfortable, at ease, to have a sense of well-being, but does not want his attention to be distracted.

Having worked out how your room will be used, you should consider what sort of finishes are going to be suitable. With food

Left: Built-in bench seating round a corner-placed table provides a lot of seating in small space. The continuation of the white and blue colour scheme also ensures that the dining area is in tune with the kitchen.

Above: This dining room is fitted into a convenient alcove and delineated by the red light, chairs and checked tablecloth as well as by its island of matting.

Right: The kitchen area is one convenient step down from the dining room with its nice use of pine, well-stocked bookshelves and gleaming wood floor. The kitchen area is tiled to continue the rustic effect.

WHERE TO EAT

Getting seated

Dining tables come in a vast range of shapes and sizes—square, round, rectangular or oval: but there are some basic rules to follow when it comes to choosing a table for a room of a particular size.

Each place setting (with an armless chair) takes about 66 cm (2 ft 3 in) with 5 cm (2 in) added to the width for chairs with arms. A long table should be at least 75 cm (2 ft 6 in) wide if both sides are to be used. Each person will need at least 75 cm (2 ft 6 in) to give space for getting in and out. And, of course, there must be an ample passageway around the table: 100 cm from table to wall is really the minimum allowance.

When buying a table and chairs, if possible spend some time sitting in the chairs *at* the table. Make sure they are a good height for the table, that any chairs with arms will fit under the table, and that seats stay supportive through long sitting sessions. Soften upright wooden or folding metal chairs with cushions if necessary, but remember this may change their height.

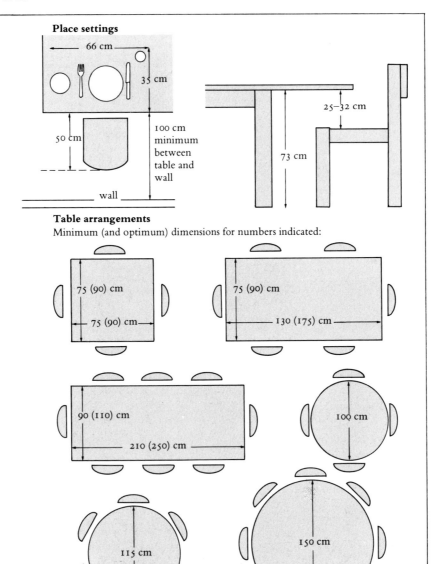

Place settings

Table arrangements
Minimum (and optimum) dimensions for numbers indicated:

around, surfaces should be as practical as possible: choose flooring which will not show crumbs and can be mopped up easily; sideboards should be provided with protective covers if they are not heatproof; traditional polished tables might look good, but with children around, you may be better off going for a heatproof, scrubbable surface which can be wiped over quickly; upholstery should be washable; wallpaper need not be as tough as the vinyl-coated varieties.

In short what you should aim to create in a dining room is a special atmosphere within a very practical framework, so when you've provided for the basics you can add to the mood with window treatments, interesting lighting and decorative tricks to make the room as comfortable, as functional and as good looking as you can.

Eating in the dining end of this extremely pretty dining-kitchen is like eating in a conservatory. Floor to ceiling glass doors and window open directly onto an equally charming paved garden. It all looks beautifully casual until you notice the careful transition from dining area tiles to garden paving with the fresh grey and white blinds as a demarcation point. Wine racks are tucked neatly and accessibly under the marble serving top with its vaguely rural wood supports.

When you know where your dining area is going to be and what size table and chairs will fit best into the space, you can start thinking about how you plan to treat the other important elements in the room—the walls, floor and windows.

Walls, floors and windows

There are any number of suitable treatments for walls in a dining room: there is not going to be much wear and tear, and no need for waterproof surfaces, as in kitchens or bathrooms so you can afford to have some fun. Paint them deep matt, eggshell or shiny gloss and hang them with pictures or a collection of some sort. Use one of the attractive paint techniques which are re-gaining popularity: spongeing, rag rolling or dragging. Stencil a border round the ceiling, around the door and windows, and above the skirting boards. Wallpaper them or cover them with fabric: felt, hessian, sacking, lining fabric or printed cotton. Panel them with wood, line them with cork, strip the plaster back to the brick; the choice is endless. Tongue-and-groove panelling will make a complete transformation: stain it, varnish it or paint it. Or finish with one of the *trompe*

l'oeil paint techniques like murals or marbling. If you do a lot of entertaining and want it to look spectacular at night then mirror tiles will gleam and sparkle and reflect candlelight beautifully.

If floorboards are in reasonable condition, they could be stripped, sanded and polished. Or they could be painted, or stencilled or both. I, personally, do not think it a very good idea to have carpet in the dining room where it only picks up smells and gets dirtier more quickly than in most places, since people do, without fail, drop things. But there is nothing against rugs of any description. Bricks, old tiles, new tiles, quarry tiles, Mexican, French or Spanish tiles, ceramic tiles, slate and even marble facing all look spectacular if you are prepared to put up with the clattering noise from chairs pulled up to the table and pushed back again. Vinyl is

A clever feature of this living/dining/guest room, left, is that half the table top can be removed and pushed against a wall when not in use. In another kitchen-diner, right, old linoleum has been painted a milky cream to go with walls, ceiling and units.

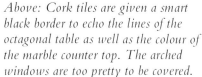

Above: Cork tiles are given a smart black border to echo the lines of the octagonal table as well as the colour of the marble counter top. The arched windows are too pretty to be covered.

Top right: Bleached boards are in keeping with the various shades of pine in a spacious country room.

Right: Grey lattice paper, silver grey paint and lavish baskets of orchids, set against botanical drawings, make this room look especially cool, airy and expensive. And with the sort of view shown here, curtains or blinds would be quite unnecessary.

practical, so is vinyl-coated cork, and lineoleum, which now comes in all colours and can be inlaid or arranged in a pattern in various shades with quite spectacular results. Black and white vinyl tiles can look particularly effective, and hardboard or chipboard, painted or varnished, make cheap cover-ups. I was always immensely impressed with the white Amtico floor we had in the dining room when my children were small. It seemed to withstand the onslaught of bicycles, tricycles and roller skates with scarcely a scratch to show.

Windows give you a chance to go to town. The obvious window treatments in traditional dining rooms are curtains on rods, or under pelmets, or hung from various headings, tied back at the sides, and used with roller, Roman or festoon blinds if you wanted to cut a particular dash. Blinds on their own can fit any atmosphere, particularly if windows are awkward, small or you did not want to lose too much light. Vertical or louvred blinds, pinoleum or matchstick blinds or Venetian blinds are more appropriate in modern settings. Add colour with roller blinds, atmosphere with Austrian blinds, or create an entirely different mood with cottagey patterned curtains. Match them with other patterns in the room.

Then there are shutters in natural or white-painted wood: if you have

Victorian shutters, strip them, and hang a pretty lace panel at the window. Close the shutters over it at night. Or have no window treatment at all except glass shelves full of plants, or plants hanging from the ceiling or from poles slung across the window. There are enormous numbers of possibilities when you get over the thought that you must have some sort of fabric at the windows.

Seeing to eat

Whatever the style of your dining room, traditional, modern or something in between, the same broad principles of lighting apply. People need to see what they're eating but the light must never be so bright that it kills any atmosphere you're trying to achieve. Although the fittings can be totally different according to the room itself, the effect should be the same: subtle lighting, capable of creating different moods but in plentiful supply over those places that need it.

Obviously the table and sideboard or carving table need to be well lit, but whether you use a light right over the table, a chandelier, candelabra or side lights, they really should be used in conjunction with a dimmer switch. If you do have a hanging light over the table it should not hang more than 85 cm to 90 cm (34 in to 36 in) from the table top. A rise-and-fall fitting ensures it will be right. This could be discreetly boost-

Window treatments for dining rooms. Top left: Grey walls, Roman blinds and a grey-covered table tucked into a panelled bay window make a pretty dining oasis. Top right: Dinner for two among a symphony of nutmeg shades in this mellow dining hall with its romantic curtains. Right: Sheer lace curtains share the same flowing fern design as the wallpaper. The bare pine table set right by the window is a cheerful breakfast or lunch place. Far right: The window treatment here reinforces the clean lines of this uncluttered dining area. The table accessories have been chosen to reflect the same colours.

ed by concealed uplights in corners, or by strip lights running round the room just below the ceiling and concealed by a pelmet or valance.

There are, of course, all sorts of chandeliers available for traditional rooms in brass, iron, wood, wrought iron and crystal, but again the effect can be discreetly boosted by recessed downlights set in the ceiling to light up the chandelier itself. This is especially effective with crystal.

To add special accent, use spots round the room to highlight pictures or fireplace, and take any collections you may have into consideration when you are planning lighting: a lit display is always very dramatic. Wallwashers, downlights or up-lighters can be used to highlight areas of the room, or sculptural halogen floor lamps with dimmers can be ready to flood a room with sunshine-like light, or give a warm and cosy glow.

Setting the table

The table setting–china, glass, cut-lery, linen–is as much a part of dining room decoration as the furni-ture and framework. There's no point in getting all the other decorat-ive details perfect if your plates and knives and forks are all wrong. It doesn't matter whether they are family heirlooms or bargains from the market stall; if they're right for the setting, that's all that counts.

China, cutlery and glass all need to

Far left: A wide-brimmed pendant light adds sparkle as well as light to the transparent table setting of glass and clear plastic beneath. Flowers stand out with clarity against the see-through surfaces and floor. Note the upright radiator in the recess.

Left: The downlight shining through the lavish indoor tree gives dramatic but subtle light to this good-looking room. Large Mexican terracotta tiles make a mellow base for the russets of the chairs and table. Note the table centre of pots of mustard and cress.

Above: Clever neon lighting above this table means that the whole feel –and colour–of the room can be changed at a touch of a switch.

95

flowers repeat colours of room

red lacquer finish walls
make room look much larger

elaborate print
napkins remniscent
of oriental fabric

cool marble
table against
the riot of
colour

brilliant
mustard yellow
curtains over black
blind add dash

light carpet
to expand space

inexpensive bentwood
chairs painted black
add to oriental air

Red, mustard and black together add dash and style to what is actually a very small room. The glossy walls and curtains help make the room look larger than it is and combine with a Burmese table and corner cupboard to give a vaguely Oriental air, which is even more apparent when the octagonal marble table is laid (above). Here the mood is continued with the black straw tablemats and the exotic napkins fanned out into the tall glasses. The chairs are basic bentwood simply glossed black to achieve an expensive-looking finish.

be useful as well as decorative. When you're choosing them think as much about shapes and sizes as about colour and pattern. Do they come in a wide range to suit all your needs? Are they going to be your serviceable everyday sets or only used on special occasions? Will they stand up to family wear and tear or look too sturdy for dinner parties? Are they all dishwasher/oven/freezer proof? Do they need to look equally at home in kitchen, dining room or living room? Do you want to be able to add to them over the years or is the

manufacturer likely to discontinue that particular pattern? Good table linen is also essential – to show off the food and add to the atmosphere. By changing cloths and napkins you can alter the feeling and style of the room quite spectacularly without going to a lot of expense – bright paper tablewear for children's parties, sophisticated damask or fine linen for a formal dinner party or cheerful gingham for casual or family meals.

One of my most favourite dining rooms was in an old country farmhouse with brick floors, uneven

nutmeg brown walls and a huge fireplace where there was almost always a fire. There was a long elm table, an old chestnut French provincial armoire, a rather well-worn 17th century velvet-covered Spanish chest and thick white cotton Roman blinds, edged with a brown and apricot cotton to match the tablecloth.

The matching or contrasting of tablecloths, napkins and window fabrics is always a pretty thing to do and by changing them you change the mood effectively at little cost.

Left: Silky festoon blinds make a sumptuous backdrop for a nicely faded wood table full of sparkle and gleaming silver. Lace mats and velvet seated Regency chairs complete the traditional dining room elegance.

Right: Breakfast by the sea, and what could be more appropriate than the blue and white china on a blue and white tablecloth under a full vase of roses. The striped rug fits quite happily into the unashamedly romantic setting which even has a flower-filled fireplace.

97

Once you have decided which facts you have to face, and whittled down the possibilities according to space, family and pocket, you can decide much more easily on the feeling you would like to introduce. Clearly, in a family dining room with several small children to cater for you are not likely to plump for any sort of exotica, or even the favourite splendours of velvet and mahogany. You are much more likely to go for old pine, or oak, tough lacquer or vinyl—at least for several years, but there is no reason why these cannot work just as well and create a feeling of their own.

Even if you don't have children, there may be other limitations that turn out to be more inhibiting than inspiring. Here's where it pays to borrow a little inspiration. Think which public places, which restaurants, in particular, have made you feel comfortable and at ease. Do you go for the opulent feel of linen, sparkle of cut glass and rich warm colouring, or do you prefer the more casual look of bare wood and brick? Do you like a clean-lined, pale wood, Scandinavian feel? The lightness of glass and wicker and white-painted plaster or brick? Or the softness of long sweeping print tablecloths and fabric-covered walls?

These days you do not have to go for matching suites of furniture in the dining room, any more than you have to go for three piece suites in the living room. No one will look askance if you have a makeshift wooden table disguised by a floor length tablecloth (with interchangeable overcloths), painted or lacquered ex-kitchen chairs, and an old dresser for a sideboard, or an old Victorian or Edwardian wardrobe for glass and china storage. Why should they? What you are achieving with such a happy mix is very much more personal and, therefore, interesting than the blandness of the careful match.

Set the mood

Colour is a useful tool to achieving a particular atmosphere: dark colours—rust, deep green, earth colours, dark woods—create a warm, inviting atmosphere

Unit furniture, spreading plants and an even more spreading Arco light, left, divide dining from living area in a long, clean-lined room. A different effect, right; a happy mix of pretty pine dresser and table, white-painted directors' chairs, old stove and cane side tables is still homogeneous.

DINING IN STYLE

and show off food well. Bright, primary colours make for a cheerful, family room. Fashionable pastels are fresh and clean for daytime eating and cool and subtle for evening atmosphere. Whatever the colour scheme, there are certain characteristic styles.

Traditional with polished wood furniture and fine accessories to create a feeling of opulence. Walls in dark, warm colours, with rich fitted carpets or traditional rugs make for a quietly splendid effect. Panelled walls enhance the atmosphere.

Farmhouse follows the style of the farmhouse kitchen, and has a pine dresser or armoire as its focal point. Traditionally, flooring is of flagstones or quarry tiles, softened by rugs or matting. Old fashioned pine tables are expensive, but you could cover a modern one with a PVC cloth in a rustic pattern for everyday use and a more prettily patterned cotton cloth for special occasions. Window treatments should be fairly simple: floral or gingham curtains with tie-backs are ideal.

Scandinavian freshness is characterised by modern pine or beech and clean lines. Colour and design are all important; plants, clear colours (but not strong primary ones) and lots of white (paint, walls, floor or accessories) help to achieve this healthy non-fussy look.

Top left: Grapefruit yellow walls, an abundance of marguerites, a spanking white floor and pale wood furniture for a Scandinavian look.

Above: Chunky furniture, black-painted bentwood chairs, matting and a cheerful garden view for a nice no-nonsense dining-living room.

Left: Up-dated traditional with slightly oriental overtones in the Chinese chairs, art, blossom trees and rattan blinds. Co-ordinated cloths, napkins and curtains owe rather more to the West.

Right: Farmhouse style furniture assisted by the charming rustic nature of the room itself.

DINING IN STYLE

Above: This is a fair approximation of French café style, with its bentwood chairs, marble-topped table and turn-of-the-century tiled floor.

Right: Not so much Hi-Tech as high ingenuity, because this dining room is actually a corridor with a mirrored wall just by the front door. Note the interesting idea of suspended spots operated by a dimmer switch.

Top, far right: Here is a touch of Eastern fantasy with the tented ceiling, kimono-style print, which is also used on the cushions, cane furniture and basketware.

Bottom, far right: Weird, wonderful and slightly film-set-ish.

Eastern fantasy runs riot with fabric decorations in either plain or delicately patterned style. Tented ceilings, fabric-covered walls, floor-length cloths and extravagant combinations of curtains and blinds at the window give a luxurious exotic feeling. Use lining fabrics for economy, trimmed with pattern border or edged with braid. If you are at home with colour and pattern, you could go for a Persian look, with patterned Indian cotton bedspreads draped round windows and tented over the table.

Thirties style cries out for a dining suite. Although this is generally considered a thing of the past, there has been a revival in the popularity of the solidly built, veneered Thirties suite with its square lines. You need panache to carry it off, with carefully selected ornaments and crockery from the period–fortunately, there's still quite a lot of it around; geometric patterned wallpaper or plain walls with a border pattern in peaches and rusts.

French café is reminiscent of the local bistro. The French are masters of restaurant cooking and atmosphere, so why not take a leaf from their book? Bentwood chairs, small circular tables and wall-mounted globe café lights are the key. Walls need to be mellow: dark creams, possibly sponged or rag rolled to give a textured effect. A dado rail, fixed round the room at the level of chair backs, with painted panelling below it will add more character.

Hi-tech says modern finishes and colours which give a bright, space-age feel. Go for angular-shaped chairs, softening them with cushions in bright, geometric prints. Trestle tables of either laminate or glass suit the wood. Flooring should be non-committal: plain, functional cord fitted carpet, or rubber stud flooring. Simple window treatments, such as vertical louvres or slick Venetian blinds are the most appropriate.

But don't be tied by necessity or convention to furnish all in one style. It is quite acceptable to mix, say, the feeling of the 17th century with the very modern; country pieces with glass and chrome; modern bentwood with early Victorian; a nice Regency side table with a scrubbed pine table. If you can't afford, or can't find, a good antique table to suit your style, get a second-hand, junk table, cover it with cloths, and invest as much as you can in comfortable chairs. Then again, you can still get a traditional feeling without having to spend money on a set of antique chairs. Old deal or pine kitchen chairs can be picked up reasonably in junk shops and painted or stained; not particularly nice reproduction chairs can be lacquered in unexpected colours. And so on.

DINING IN STYLE

Stylish transformations
As well as these pointers to distinctive style, there are many finishing touches which will add personality to a dining room, whether it is newly decorated, or a dining room you can't afford to re-vamp (or don't want to re-decorate, because it is in a rented home).

Put in a dado rail round the room, level with the backs of the chairs: it will protect the wallcovering, and change the proportions of the room. Polish it, or paint it to match the woodwork.

Fireplaces with real fires can be awkward in a very small dining room. Go for background heat, which is more controllable, and put an arrangement of dried flowers in the redundant grate.

Cover the walls with large panels of fabric—wall hangings, rugs or (appropriately) tablecloths. Staple them in place or stretch them on battens.

Add light to a room, and increase its apparent size by putting up mirror tiles (or fixing panels of mirror) in alcoves.

Make the room an extension of the garden by keeping potted plants by the window. Patio plants can be moved to 'winter over' in the dining room. Windowsills serve as greenhouse staging.

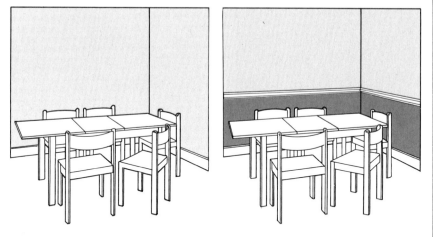

a plain dining room (above left) given character by adding a dado rail (above right) or covering the walls with panels of fabric (below).

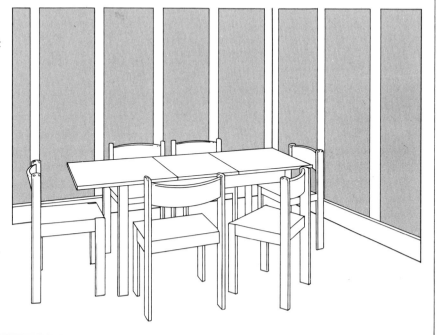

The collector's room
Because of the nature of the furnishings in a dining room (a large, flat surface, empty walls) and because it is needed to serve its purpose only at regular, specified times during the day (meal times), it is an ideal room to serve as a collector's library. Collections can be displayed and made into a decorative asset, and if you are a serious collector you can use the room as a quiet retreat to pursue your hobby, cleaning or mending plates, checking hallmarks on silver, valuing new purchases from relevant text books, cataloguing details—whatever might be involved in your particular field.

● Use wire plate hangers to hang a collection of plates on the walls, grouped according to colour, size or origin.

● Line the walls with shelves to house a library of books or magazines.

● Build storage cabinets and shelves to hold a collection of records.

● Display a collection of models—houses, soldiers, toys, cars—on shelves, carefully lit by strip lights behind baffles.

● Frame a collection of samplers—or something more unusual like lace collars or handkerchieves (or table napkins), and hang them in groups on the wall.

real candles in
candelabra and sconces

Regency column
and bust

wood glued
to produce
'gothic' shape

pediment is
actually hardboard

inexpensive
muslin curtain
with quality trim

'lace' is
cut out
paper

dado panelling,
door and cabinet
(inset) painted
for 'oak graining'
effect

Regency
fire-screen

genuine Regency
table and chairs

*A graceful Regency dining room in
which period features, such as the
dado, with its 'faux bois' oak-grained
treatment, have been restored for effect.
The candle-lit candelabra and chairs
are genuine but the curtains and
skirting board heating are welcome
modern introductions. The equally
modern cabinet (inset) is ingeniously
aged with paper 'lace' and a hardboard
pediment.*

Dining room proper

The style of this dining room is a very successful mix: the furniture is modern and so is the sculptural halogen floor lamp but the general effect and feel is formal and traditional, even rather Victorian. The walls set the tone and the theme. They have been lacquered an Indian red and panelled over with lengths of an Indian red and cream paper. A matching fabric is used for the overcloth on the table. The same colours are followed through at the window with its Indian red curtains edged with cream and its cream blind. This time the undercloth of the table matches the curtains. Chairs, sideboard and halogen lamp are all a glossy black. And just as the lamp adds height to one corner of the room, so the pedestal, urn and oversize fern balance the effect and do the same in the opposite corner. Lighting is all important here. A subdued background light comes from strip light running all the way round the room just under the ceiling but concealed by a pelmet papered in the wall design. The halogen lamp with its own dimmer gives whatever extra light is required. An uplight behind the pedestal shines through the leaves of the plant to create quite a different effect of gently diffused light.

Above: Terracotta-coloured painted boards in this dining room make a spectacular background for part of a collection of blue and white china. There is more of it on the table which is given additional emphasis by the blue and white chair covers. Note too, the interesting barley-sugar twist candlesticks and the old chest. The russet colour is the perfect complement to the blue/white scheme.

Right: The vivid painting clearly dominates everything else in a small red lacquered room and not only dictates the other colours, for example in the flowers and rug, but also the slightly tropical feel of the table, napkins and chairs.

● Collect old kitchen equipment—
bread boards, wicker carpet beaters,
jelly moulds—and hang them on the
walls.

● Put up a pin board and start a
collection of cards from restaurants.
Each time you visit a new eating
place, pick up a card, write your
verdict on the back, and pin it on the
board for future reference.

● Display your children's art lesson
masterpieces round the room—it
will encourage and gratify them and
will certainly provide talking points.

● Certain collections—Mickey
Mouse ephemera or period mem-
orabilia need a range of different
treatments to display them to their
best advantage: dot pictures and
plaques round the wall, arrange toys
and crockery on shelves, lay rugs on
the floor. Even the table setting can
be part of the collection.

● Collect something that you can
actually use: a collection of cruets is
both amusing and practical; give
each guest a different set to use.

Whatever your collection, display it
thoughtfully. Try to give pride of
place to one prized item: maybe the
most valuable, or the most spectacular, perhaps the very *first* of your
collection, or the one that was a
special gift or heirloom.

Position it in the centre of the
mantelpiece, stand it on a shelf on its

own, shine a spotlight on to it, or
hang it on an empty wall where it
will attract attention.

Clever lighting can make all the
difference to the look of a collection,
drawing attention to it and showing
it off to its best advantage at the same
time. The kind of fixtures that are
best for this sort of accent lighting
are the various types of spotlights,
wallwashers, pinhole or framing

projectors, as well as uplights and
candles. If you are lighting a single
object, aim to place your fixture so
that there is no distracting reflection.
You need to experiment, lighting
from above, or below or straight on,
to see which gives the best effect.
Glass shelves are often particularly
effective, especially when set in a
mirrored alcove, and lit from above
or below, or both.

*Above: Almost everything else is
subjugated to the neatly arranged
collection of art in this dining room
where both decor and furniture are
firmly restrained. The long glass table
is dramatic but not distracting and the
only other colours are in the plant life
and the mahogany-finish arched door
frame. Note too, how everything in
the room—table, chairs, all the
pictures—is framed in steel.*

I like to think that one can make provision to eat almost anywhere in the home, just as one should be able to move small tables about to different parts of the garden. It is obviously nice to be able to eat in the kitchen or in the living room. But why not the hall for a change? The bedroom for a breakfast *à deux* or cosy supper? Even in the bathroom –if you happen to have sufficient space, and money, for a luxurious bathroom/exercise room, bathroom/study, bathroom/ sitting room, bathroom/ bedroom–you could fit in a small health bar with fruit and vitamin drinks.

All you need is a table and chairs that do not look out of place in whatever room they are put– though, of course, folding varieties of both can be brought out for the occasion.

In any case, in any home where space is at a premium, you have to learn to use that space for all it's worth. If you do not have the luxury of a dining room used just for dining–and most of us do not, the trick is to make your dining table look as if it is not a dining table most of the time. And that means that you do not have a table surrounded by chairs–except, of course, when you are actually going to use it for eating.

Dining/work room

If you use what was the dining room for a work room/study as well, you should either have a round table which can be piled with books when necessary, a table set off-centre, or a drop-leaf table that can be pulled out and set up in the centre of the room as required. All of them can then double as a desk, homework table, sewing or drawing table. If you occasionally have quite big parties it would be worth buying a table with extra leaves (store them under a bed, or behind a door). Bookshelves can have cupboards underneath to take china, glass, cutlery and table linen as well as files, stationery and normal work room apparatus. It is just a question of organization. Keep the breakfront surface (the top of the cupboard part) about twice as deep as the shelves above, and you will have a ready-made serving area for meals as well as an effective room divider.

This small study/dining room, left, is thoroughly light-hearted with its floor like an abstract painting and its delicious stripy fabric. White dining table and chairs blend happily into this chunky white living room, right, with its dividing chimney breast.

DUAL-PURPOSE DINING AREAS

Another great aid to any part-time dining area is the trolley or serving cart which makes the valuable link between kitchen and eating area, and is useful for transportation of food and dishes, and in addition provides storage and an extra serving surface.

The problem of where to put all those extra chairs is not really so very difficult. There are several solutions. For example in a flat or apartment, you could buy chairs that would act as occasional chairs; have them covered in the sort of colour that will go in every room and they can then be distributed throughout bedrooms, living rooms, hall if it is big enough, and brought together as and when needed.

Alternatively, you could buy folding chairs that could either be put away in, say, a hall cupboard and taken out when needed, or hung on a wall. The clear perspex or plexiglass variety will take very little visual space since you can look right through them and the brightly coloured wooden varieties are a decoration in themselves, looking rather like modern sculptures against the wall's surface.

This kitchen/dining room, with its useful draughtsman-like table and mobile chairs, works equally efficiently as an office. Altogether a practical, useful room.

magistretti chair

plia chair

modern movement
tubular steel chair

medici chair

wheelback chair

director's chair

bauhaus chair

wicker chair

bentwood chair

DUAL-PURPOSE DINING AREAS

Dining/guest rooms

Much the same suggestions can apply to a room that also acts as part-time guest room. Here, of course, you will also need to make provision for a bed and clothes storage. The bed could either be a sofa bed or a studio couch with, perhaps, extra drawers underneath, or, in a smaller room, an armchair that transforms itself into a bed. The bed/storage area could be neatly screened off with matchstick blinds.

If at all possible, you should provide a wardrobe either by having a wall of storage with shelves, drawers and cupboards to take both dining accessories and clothes, or by having a separate armoire or old wardrobe (which can also take silver, china, glass etc.). And there is almost no limit to the ways you can reorganize the space in some of those old Victorian and Edwardian ward-robes that can still be found. Even with dire shortage of cash and space, hooks fixed on the back of the door will take an overnight clothes hanger or two.

If you wanted to make the room seem more like a bedroom/sitting room than a study/library/dining room that will also accommodate a guest, you could make much more of the sofa bed and have a rectang-ular or drop-leaf table like a sofa table behind it. This can then be pulled out and opened out as the occasion demands.

Living/dining rooms

This is a pretty usual arrangement nowadays, and again the trick is to disguise the dining table when not in use for dining. Round tables and drop-leafs can be bought to act as library tables and sofa tables as described above, or there are large adjustable coffee and cocktail tables which can be raised to dining or lowered to coffee table height as desired.

Table tops can also be concealed within a storage wall in much the same way as a Murphy bed, so that the leaf can be pulled down when wanted and shut up later to look like a piece of smooth wall. Or, more ingeniously, the underside can be mirrored so that when it is flipped up it will look for all the world like a large looking glass.

Obviously, tables can be a visible part of a storage wall, acting as either a desk or for dining, and some of them have an extendable top so that they can be pulled right out when you have company.

If you have a dining alcove in your living room you could make the division more complete by building a low storage wall of shelves or cupboards with plenty of room inside for all your dining equipment and serving space on top. Or you could line the walls with book-shelves with cupboards underneath to provide storage and serving space, as in the dining/workroom.

Alcoves like this can also be treated like separate small rooms and lined with mirror or mirror tiles; or with the curtain or shade fabric; or painted or papered in a colour out of the room which is at the same time different from the main walls. Any cloths used on the table could be made from the same fabric as the main room curtains or upholstery.

Above: In this living room the round table under the large pine mirror is perfect for dining and looks just as good when it is not laid for a meal. The handsome 19th century chairs can be used as occasional seating in other parts of the room.

Right: A kitchen/dining room with a distinctly conservatory feel.

Eating in the hall

Modern wallpaper in an old American design is used for this entrance hall and makes a gentle background for eating. Its blue leaves dictate the colours for carpet and archway curtain. A paler patterned cotton with the same colouring but in a different design is used as an overcloth over a donkey-brown felt tablecloth. The skirting or base boards are also painted blue and the ceiling colour catches the background of the paper as well. French Provençal chairs with cane seats are light and elegant and stand against the wall when the tablecloths are removed and the dropleaf oval table contracts to its daytime size to become a side table set underneath the mirror. The large expanses of staircase wall are perfect for displaying the miscellany of differently sized prints, paintings, drawings and mirrors in a massed effect rather than marching up the stairs. This sort of ambitious arrangement has tremendous impact but must be done with great precision if it is not to look a haphazard jumble. All the preliminary juggling with shapes and sizes should be done with the art set out on the floor. A dimmer switch controls the recessed downlights in the ceiling and creates a dining island at night.

DUAL-PURPOSE DINING AREAS

If the alcove is very narrow, use an upholstered bench with suspended cushions for back rests on one side of the table and chairs on the other.

If the style of the main room will take it, a dining alcove can sometimes be semi-curtained off as in a box at the theatre or in one of those titillating little areas off famous turn-of-the-century Paris restaurants used for discreet entertaining.

When there is no separate alcove or eating area allowed for, a distinct dining place can be made by raising a table on a plywood platform at whatever height is preferred. Again, it can be separated a little from the mainstream area with a low wall of cupboards and shelves, or, providing the main area is big enough, a high wall of shelves.

If, of course, the room is quite big, all sorts of divider devices can be used to partition off a dining area, from screens of one sort or another to large indoor plants or trees.

Another good solution for dining if the room will take it, is a long old refectory table which, like the library table idea, can be used for piling books and magazines on, for displaying flowers and objects and to provide both work and eating surfaces.

Dining halls

A nice wide hall is a natural for dining, and again, the table should be an object in its own right, in use for

Left: The dark gate-legged table at the dining end of this all-white living room looks just as charming devoid of chairs, which can be easily folded away when not in use.

Top right: Although long and narrow, the space in this open-plan kitchen-dining-living area has been cleverly planned and furnished. The kitchen area towards the garden crams in most necessities including adequate storage, and the round table can act as a desk as well as dining table. Note the Plia chairs stacked neatly by the garden door.

Bottom right: Landings, if they're a reasonable size and shape, can make good dining areas too. This space, somewhat exotically divided from the living area by what looks like a christening font, makes a very pleasant place for eating, for sitting chatting or even for playing cards.

Far right: Sometimes, squeezing in dining space is more a matter of courage than anything else. One could hardly imagine a table for six in this tiny bedsitting room (the bed is up the other end), but it works. And pushed against the wall when not in use for dining, the table makes an excellent desk/work surface as well.

display and general dumping space when not in use for eating. If you are lucky enough to have full length cupboards in the hallway, they can easily be reorganized to take china, cutlery, glass and linen and maybe even a trolley or serving cart.

Small tables for two can make very good use of the wasted space at the end of a corridor. Good lighting, a picture or two or a rug fixed to the end wall will give a whole new lease of life to what could have been a boring dead end.

Dining/kitchens

There is no doubt that eating in the kitchen has an attraction all its own. It is more informal, warmer somehow (both in fact as well as in atmosphere), and, naturally, there is no feeling of separation from the action or the cook, for whom, of course, it is also more practical. Many more dishes can be made that go direct from stove to table than could ever be produced for a separate dining room or area.

It's important to have enough space and a well-thought out arrangement that allows both eating and cooking to take place without the one interfering with the other. The cook needs room to get at the cooker, sink and cupboards without hindrance and to move around the kitchen comfortably. Lots of worktops and dumping space is essential. It's more pleasant for the diners too

if the cooking paraphernalia – dirty pans and plates – can be kept out of sight

So if the kitchen is large enough to take any sort of eating surface – even if it is only an extension of a counter top to make a breakfast and supper bar, this is obviously a bonus. If

breakfast is a cut-and-run meal then a bar counter is a good idea and a nice compromise between setting a proper table and snatching a cup of coffee on the wing. And children enjoy perching on stools. But you still have to decide whether you want to make a kitchen you can eat

There is a very clever use of space in this kitchen-dining-family room. The central green tiled island unit, here laid for supper, acts as dining table and is also the main work surface. Every surface is used for cupboard space including the area over the island unit as well as beneath it.

The right setting for the right room. A round skirted table makes a pleasant place for breakfast (and supper too) by the window seat in a country bedroom, top, far left. Two trestle tables, placed end to end, provide generous dining or work space in this celadon green living room, bottom, far left. Hallways can be dramatic places to eat in, especially a soaring space like this one, top left, where the hexagonal marbled table is echoed in the dinner service. Once candles are lit the table becomes an oasis, as here in the room shown bottom left. Wherever there is space for a table and chairs, there is space for a dining area. This landing, below, by French doors makes a pretty indoor/outdoor dining space.

DUAL-PURPOSE DINING AREAS

Left: The dining corner of this basement living room comes straight up against the kitchen alcove and uses the half partition wall for a wraparound seating support. Shutters on the bay window are painted in an abstract design to match other colours in the room.

Above: The dining area counter top of this apricot and white room acts as a kind of visual partition.

Right: The eating area is divided off from the working part of this kitchen by an island of matting and a nicely detailed window treatment with green edged scalloped pelmet and green checked shade to match the chair seats and napkins.

in, or an eating place which is also the kitchen. There is quite a difference.

Either way, you will probably want to put more emphasis on decoration than you would do normally. You could, for example, divide the table area off from the working area with a storage/serving wall or the sort of peninsular unit described in Chapter 2. Or you could install some sort of screen, dividing panel, a blind that lets down from the ceiling, and even a stack of wine racks which would make a substantial and permanent wall in themselves. You could too, choose rather different wall treatments for the dining part: flame-proofed fabric; wallpaper, a warm, dark paint, and add pictures, prints, objects, favourite collections, bookshelves, anything that emphasises that the space is as much for living as for working in.

Use pretty table cloths and napkins. Go for well-designed china that delights the eye and sets off the food. Pay attention to plants and flowers and make sure that you have your lighting on dimmer switches so that you can dim it right down for dining as well as drawing a veil over any kitchen clutter.

In fact, if you always bear in mind that once a table is set for dining, lights lowered, candles lit, that table becomes an oasis, complete in itself, you can make a dining room wherever the table is.

KITCHENS & DINING ROOMS

Accent lighting Decorative lighting which is used to draw attention to chosen objects, and to create moods and highlights.

Acoustic tiles Ceiling tiles which absorb sound. They are made from pre-finished slotted insulation board or from polystyrene or fibreglass.

Architrave A moulded or decorated band framing a panel or an opening such as a door or window.

Baffle A narrow screen or partition placed so as to hinder or control the passage of light or sound.

Batterie de cuisine The whole range of utensils used in the kitchen for the preparation and cooking of food.

Butcher block A continuous run of thick wood, or a wooden block with legs, such as butchers use in butchers shops. Both are useful for chopping and preparing meat and vegetables.

Café curtain A short curtain hung from a rod going half way across a window, as in French cafés. It is some-times hung in a double tier, and is a useful treatment for windows that open inwards or face the street.

Ceramic tiles Fired clay tiles with a very hard-wearing glaze. There is a large range of colours, patterns, textures and sizes.

Corian A marble-like plastic substance used for sinks and worktops. It can be moulded to form a continuous work surface, and is durable and almost completely stain-resistant.

Cornice A decorative, horizontal band of plaster, metal or wood used to surmount a wall.

Dado The lower part of a wall separated by a rail known as the dado rail.

Dimmer switch A knob (or rheostat) or panel that is used to control bright-ness of light. It saves energy as well as giving a flexible range of lighting levels.

Downlights Fittings which can be mounted on, or recessed into a ceiling to cast pools of light onto the surface below. Most are fitted with an anti-glare device, and the direction of light can be controlled with a baffle (q.v.).

Dragging A paint technique which gives a subtle effect to a large wall surface. Paint is applied in a thin wash in vertical strokes with an almost dry brush in a contrasting shade.

Ephemera A collection of objects, not necessarily valuable, such as old posters and theatre programmes.

Ergonomics The study of work pat-terns and conditions, in order to achieve maximum efficiency.

Framing projector A light fitting whose beam can be shaped accurately so that a given surface, such as a painting or table top, can be lit exactly.

Galley kitchen Small and narrow, like the kitchen in a ship or boat.

Grouting Filling up or finishing joints between tiles with a thin mortar.

Hi-tech Contemporary style adapting industrial components for domestic use.

Hob The surface on which pans are heated. It is sometimes separate from the oven, and set into a work top.

Laminate A very strong multi-layered material such as Formica.

Marbling A paint technique which gives a veined, marble-like appearance to a surface.

Matchstick (or pinoleum) blind A blind made with fine wooden sticks which are stitched together.

Mexican tiles Ceramic tiles whose colours and patterns are inspired by traditional Mexican designs.

Murphy bed A bed that lets down from the wall against which it is con-cealed when not in use.

Pegboard A board perforated with holes from which pegs can be attached. Can be used in the kitchen for hanging utensils.

Pelmet or valance A decorative, horizontal band of fabric usually attached to the top of the window frame or just above, to hide rods and provide added interest.

Pendant lighting Lights which hang from the ceiling.

Peninsular unit A unit that juts out into a room and can be approached from three sides.

Pin-board A board, usually made from cork, on which papers or pictures can be attached with pins.

Pinhole lighting A spotlight fitting through which a narrow beam of light is projected, the beam spreading widely downwards.

Quarry tiles Fired tiles made from unrefined clays which provide very durable flooring. They are impervious to grease and liquids, and come in a range of muted colours.

Rag-rolling A paint technique in which the top coat of paint is partly removed while still wet with a roll of cloth, to reveal the base coat in a contrasting shade.

Refectory table A long narrow dining table.

Rise-and-fall fitting Used to adjust the height of a pendant lamp, especially when it hangs over a dining table.

Roman blind A blind which draws up into neat horizontal folds by means of cords threaded through rings at regular intervals to the back of the fabric. On heavy fabrics, light battens can be attached to keep the folds crisp.

Spongeing A paint technique which gives a soft speckled effect. A sponge is used to stipple paint onto a base coat in a contrast colour.

Stencil A decorative design which is cut out of waxed paper or acetate, then reproduced onto a surface below with paint using a stencil brush or spray can.

Tongue-and-groove panelling Wood panelling, where the boards are interlocked along the edges.

Track lighting A length of track along which a number of light fittings can be positioned and supplied by one electrical outlet. It can be mounted on any wall or ceiling surface, or recessed.

Trompe l'oeil Anything which de-ceives the eye.

Uplights Accent lights which are placed on the floor. They can be con-cealed behind sofas and plants to give dramatic effects.

Valance see Pelmet.

Venetian blind A pull-up blind made with horizontal slats that can be ad-justed to let in or exclude light.

Wallwashers Angled downlights (q.v.) which bathe the wall surface in light.

Work triangle An imaginary line link-ing the three main work areas around the sink, cooker and fridge.

Yacht varnish A boat varnish which gives a very resilient finish.

125

ACKNOWLEDGMENTS

The author and publishers would particularly like to thank the following people and companies for their contribution to this book;

for their invaluable help and research work: Pamela Gough, Virginia Bredin

for technical advice: David Champion, Deborah Evans, Shirley Heron

for allowing us to photograph their homes: Glynn & Carrie Boyd Harte, Catherine & Jonathan Giles, Dieter Klein, Sandy Kom Losy, Judith & Graeme Robertson, Chris Searle & Anna Southall,

for supplying merchandise for the room sets: Amtico, Cole & Son Ltd, Coriam Ltd, Marks & Spencer plc, Paris Ceramics, Rye Tiles, Sekers Fabrics Ltd, Tidmarsh & Son Ltd, Tile Mart, Tissunique Ltd, Waldorf Carpets, World's End Tiles & Flooring Ltd

for supplying props for special photography: Marks & Spencer plc, ICTC

Special photography

Jon Bouchier 16 (designer Jonathan Giles), 21, 29 left and right (designer Judith Robertson), 32 (designer Dieter Klein), 52 below left, 60 left and right (designer Lenny), 74, 82, 84, 94 (designer Jonathan Giles), 96 left and right.

Jessica Strang 28 above right, 95 left, 105 left and right (designer Boyd Harte), 114.

The publishers would like to thank the following organizations and individuals for their kind permission to reproduce the photographs in this book: Allmilmö Kitchens 37, 59, 63, 86; Alno Kitchens 52 below centre, 61 above and below left and above right; B & Q DIY Supercentres 33; Jon Bouchier/EWA 28 below centre, 118; Michael Boys/Susan Griggs Agency Ltd 53 above, 103 above, 108 left, 111; Richard Bryant 75; Camera Press 52 above right, 62, 78 left, 91, 123; Steve Colby/EWA 52 above left, 98; Cover Plus Paints 17; Dulux Paints 100 above left; Michael Dunne 11, 14, 28 above left, 30 above right, 34, 35 above left, 39 left, 41, 51, 71, 78 right, 85, 87 right, 90, 93 above right, 95 right, 97 right, 102 right, 108 right, 110, 115, 120, 121 below centre; Du Pont (UK) Ltd. 30 below right, 81 right; c. Peter M. Fine 1983 93 above left; Christine Hanscomb 22; Nelson Hargreaves 72, 121 above right; Clive Helm/EWA 14 right, 30 left, 35 below left (designer Behrens), 45 right, 73 left (designer Johnny Grey), 100 above right; Frank Herholdt 70, Frank Herholdt/EWA 100 below left; John Hill 31, 101; Ken Kirkwood 25 right, 103 below; Neil Lorimer/EWA 24, 47, 92 above left; William Mason 25 left; Moben Kitchens 8, 36, 79 below right; Nairn Floors 80; Michael Nicholson/EWA 20 above right (designer Virginia Bates), 39 right, 40 (designer Piero di Monzi), 89 (designer Leila Corbett), 99 (designer Maggi Henry), 119 above left (designer Walker/Wright), 119 below left, and right, 121 below right, 122 right; Osborne and Little 121 above left; Malcolm Robertson 23, 79 above left; Arthur Sanderson Ltd 93 below left; Jessica Strang 9, 28 below left (designer Ken Grange), 45 below left (designer Antonia Graham), 64 above right, 73, 97 left, 102 left, 109; Tim Street-Porter/EWA 20 below left (designer Joan Sachs), 48, 79 below left, 122 left; Sunway Blinds Ltd. 81 left, 93 below right; Friedhelm Thomas/EWA 6, 87 left; Jerry Tubby/EWA 10 (designer Igor Cicin Sain), 58 above left, 79 above right (designer Isabel Czarska); Transworld Feature Syndicate 20 above left, 45 above left, 46, 49, 92 below right (Elyse Lewin), 121 below left; Elizabeth Whiting Associates 92 above right; Winchmore Kitchens 50, 53 below, 58 below left and right, 61 below right, 64 below right; Wrighton Kitchens 64 left, 65, 68, 69, 112.

Black and white line illustrations by Stuart Perry. Colour illustrations by Ross Wardle/Tudor Art Studios.

INDEX